psychopth
free

psychopth
free

Recovering from Emotionally
Abusive Relationships with
Narcissists, Sociopaths,
and Other Toxic People

Jackson MacKenzie

BERKLEY BOOKS, NEW YORK

Berkley
An imprint of Penguin Random House LLC
375 Hudson Street, New York, New York 10014

Library of Congress Cataloging-in-Publication Data

MacKenzie, Jackson.
Psychopath free : recovering from emotionally abusive relationships
with narcissists, sociopaths, and other toxic people / Jackson MacKenzie.
p.   cm.
ISBN 978-0-425-27999-1
1. Psychological abuse.   2. Psychopaths—Family relationships.
3. Interpersonal relations.   I. Title.
RC569.5.P75M33   2015   2015018842
616.89'14—dc23

PUBLISHING HISTORY
Berkley trade paperback edition / September 2015

PRINTED IN THE UNITED STATES OF AMERICA

20   19   18   17   16   15   14   13

Cover design by Diana Kolsky.
Interior text design by Laura K. Corless.

Penguin
Random
House

Connect

psychopathfree.com

facebook.com/psychopathfree

twitter.com/psychopathfree

Dedicated to the Constants in my life.
Thank you for restoring my faith
in the goodness of people.

No hurt survives for long without our help, she said & then she kissed me & sent me out to play again for the rest of my life.

—Brian Andreas, *StoryPeople*

Contents

Introduction

An Adventure

Finding yourself involved with a psychopath is an adventure, that's for sure. It will open your eyes to human nature, our broken society, and, perhaps most important of all, your own spirit. It's a dark journey that will throw you into spells of depression, rage, and loneliness. It will unravel your deepest insecurities, leaving you with a lingering emptiness that haunts your every breath.

But ultimately, it will heal you.

You will become stronger than you could ever imagine. You will understand who you are truly meant to be. And in the end, you will be glad it happened.

No one ever believes me about that last part. At least, not at first. But I promise you, it's an adventure worth taking. One that will change your life forever.

So what is a psychopath? How about a narcissist or a sociopath? They're manipulative people—completely devoid of empathy—

who intentionally cause harm to others without any sense of remorse or responsibility. And despite some differences between each disorder, the bottom line is that their relationship cycles can be predicted like clockwork: Idealize, Devalue, Discard.

Years ago, this cycle had me thinking I'd never be happy again. Falling in love had somehow wiped out my entire sense of self. Instead of being joyful and trusting, I had become an unrecognizable mess of insecurities and anxiety.

But life is a lot of fun these days—mostly just running around outside in my bathing suit and eating pizza. And this is all thanks to a lucky Google search that led me to psychopathy, which led me to the friends who saved my life, which led us to cofound a tiny online recovery community, which now reaches millions of survivors every month!

At PsychopathFree.com, we see new members join every single day, always with a seemingly hopeless and all-too-familiar tale. Left feeling lost and broken, they wonder if they will ever find happiness again.

One year later, that person is nowhere to be found.

In his or her place, there is a beautiful stranger who stands tall and helps others out from the shadows. A stranger who takes pride in their own greatest qualities: empathy, compassion, and kindness. A stranger who speaks of self-respect and boundaries. A stranger who practices introspection in order to better conquer their own demons.

So what happened in that year?

Well, a lot of good stuff. So much that I had to write a book. I might be biased—actually, I definitely am—but I think PsychopathFree.com has one of the coolest healing processes out there.

We believe in education, open dialogue, validation, and self-discovery. We have a uniquely inspiring user base, full of resilient values and honest friendships.

Yes, friendships. Because this journey is personal, but it's also remarkably universal. Whether it be a whirlwind romance, a scheming coworker, an abusive family member, or a life-consuming affair, a relationship with a psychopath is always the same. Your mind is left spinning. You feel worthless and lost. You become numb to the things that once made you happy.

I cannot fix a toxic relationship (because toxic people cannot change), but I can give you a new place to start. And I can promise that you will feel joy again. You will learn to trust your intuition. You will walk this world with the wisdom of a survivor and the gentle wonder of a dreamer.

But first, you'll need to forget everything you thought you knew about people. Understanding psychopathy requires letting go of your basic emotional instincts. Remember, these are people who prey on forgiveness. They thrive on your need for closure. They manipulate compassion and exploit sympathy.

Since the dawn of time, psychopaths have waged psychological warfare on others—humiliating and shaming kind, unsuspecting victims—people who never asked for it; people who aren't even aware of the war until it's over.

But this is all about to change.

So say farewell to love triangles, cryptic letters, self-doubt, and manufactured anxiety. You will never again find yourself desperately awaiting a text from the person you love. You will never again censor your spirit for fear of losing the "perfect" relationship. You will never again be told to stop overanalyzing something that urgently needs analysis. You are no longer a pawn in the mind games of a psychopath. You are free.

And now it's time for your adventure.

Love,
Jackson

Spotting Toxic People

Your strengthened intuition is the greatest defense against a manipulative person. It is a skill that can never be exploited— and once learned, it will serve you a lifetime.

30 Red Flags

There are a lot of phenomenal studies on the traits and characteristics of psychopaths. A quick Internet search will lead you to them. The red flags in this book are intended to supplement these resources.

So what's different about this list? Well, for one, it's specifically about relationships. But it's also about you. Each point requires introspection and self-awareness. Because if you want to spot toxic people, you cannot focus entirely on their behavior—that's only half the battle. You must also come to recognize the looming red flags in your own heart. Then you will be ready for anything.

1. **Gaslighting and crazy-making.** They blatantly deny their own manipulative behavior and ignore evidence when confronted with it. They become dismissive and critical if you attempt to disprove their fabrications with facts.

Instead of them actually addressing their inappropriate behavior, somehow it always becomes *your* fault for being "sensitive" and "crazy." Toxic people condition you to believe that the problem isn't the abuse itself, but instead your reactions to their abuse.

2. **Cannot put themselves in your shoes, or anyone else's, for that matter**. You find yourself desperately trying to explain how they might feel if you were treating them this way, and they just stare at you blankly. You slowly learn not to communicate your feelings with them, because you're usually met with silence or annoyance.

3. **The ultimate hypocrite.** "Do as I say, not as I do." They have extremely high expectations for fidelity, respect, and adoration. After the idealization phase, they will give none of this back to you. They will cheat, lie, criticize, and manipulate. But you are expected to remain perfect, otherwise you will promptly be replaced and deemed unstable.

4. **Pathological lying and excuses.** There is always an excuse for everything, even things that don't require excusing. They make up lies faster than you can question them. They constantly blame others—it is never their fault. They spend more time rationalizing their behavior than improving it. Even when caught in a lie, they express no remorse or embarrassment. Oftentimes, it almost seems as if they *wanted* you to catch them.

5. **Focuses on your mistakes and ignores their own.** If they're two hours late, don't forget that you were once five

minutes late to your first date. If you point out their inappropriate behavior, they will always be quick to turn the conversation back on you. You might begin to adopt perfectionist qualities, very aware that any mistake can and will be used against you.

6. **You find yourself explaining the basic elements of human respect to a full-grown man or woman.** Normal people understand fundamental concepts like honesty and kindness. Psychopaths often appear to be childlike and innocent, but don't let this mask fool you. No adult should need to be told how he or she is making other people feel.

7. **Selfishness and a crippling thirst for attention.** They drain the energy from you and consume your entire life. Their demand for adoration is insatiable. You thought you were the only one who could make them happy, but now you feel that anyone with a beating pulse could fit the role. However, the truth is: no one can fill the void of a psychopath's soul.

8. **Accuses you of feeling emotions that they are intentionally provoking.** They call you jealous after blatantly flirting with an ex—often done over social networking for the entire world to see. They call you needy after intentionally ignoring you for days on end. They use your manufactured reactions to garner sympathy from other targets, trying to prove how "hysterical" you've become. You probably once considered yourself to be an exceptionally easygoing per-

son, but an encounter with a psychopath will (temporarily) turn that notion upside down.

9. **You find yourself playing detective.** It's never happened in any other relationship, but suddenly you're investigating the person you once trusted unconditionally. If they're active on Facebook, you start scrolling back years on their posts and albums. Same with their ex. You're seeking answers to a feeling you can't quite explain.

10. **You are the only one who sees their true colors.** No matter what they do, they always seem to have a fan club cheering for them. The psychopath uses these people for money, resources, and attention—but the fan club won't notice, because this person strategically distracts them with shallow praise. Psychopaths are able to maintain superficial friendships far longer than relationships.

11. **You fear that any fight could be your last.** Normal couples argue to resolve issues, but psychopaths make it clear that negative conversations will jeopardize the relationship, especially ones regarding their behavior. Any of your attempts to improve communication will typically result in the silent treatment. You apologize and forgive quickly, otherwise you know they'll lose interest in you.

12. **Slowly and steadily erodes your boundaries.** They criticize you with a condescending, joking sort of attitude. They smirk when you try to express yourself. Teasing becomes the primary mode of communication in your relationship. They subtly belittle your intelligence and abilities. If you

point this out, they call you sensitive and crazy. You might begin to feel resentful and upset, but you learn to push away those feelings in favor of maintaining the peace.

13. **They withhold attention and undermine your self-esteem.** After once showering you with nonstop attention and admiration, they suddenly seem completely bored by you. They treat you with silence and become very annoyed that you're interested in continuing the passionate relationship that *they* created. You begin to feel like a chore to them.

14. **They expect you to read their mind.** If they stop communicating with you for several days, it's your fault for not knowing about the plans they never told you about. There will always be an excuse that makes them out to be the victim to go along with this. They make important decisions about the relationship and they inform everyone except you.

15. **You feel on edge around this person, but you still want them to like you.** You find yourself writing off most of their questionable behavior as accidental or insensitive, because you're in constant competition with others for their attention and praise. They don't seem to care when you leave their side—they can just as easily move on to the next source of energy.

16. **An unusual number of "crazy" people in their past.** Any ex-partner or friend who did not come crawling back to them will likely be labeled jealous, bipolar, an alcoholic, or

some other nasty smear. Make no mistake: they will speak about you the same way to their next target.

17. **Provokes jealousy and rivalries while maintaining their cover of innocence.** They once directed all of their attention to you, which makes it especially confusing when they begin to withdraw and focus on other people. They do things that constantly make you doubt your place in their heart. If they're active on social media, they'll bait previously denounced exes with old songs, photos, and inside jokes. They attend to the "competition's" activity and ignore yours.

18. **Idealization, love-bombing, and flattery.** When you first meet, things move extremely fast. They tell you how much they have in common with you—how perfect you are for them. Like a chameleon, they mirror your hopes, dreams, and insecurities in order to form an immediate bond of trust and excitement. They constantly initiate communication and seem to be fascinated with you on every level. If you have a Facebook page, they might plaster it with songs, compliments, poems, and inside jokes.

19. **Compares you to everyone else in their life.** They compare you to ex-lovers, friends, family members, and your eventual replacement. When idealizing, they make you feel special by telling you how much better you are than these people. When devaluing, they use these comparisons to make you feel jealous and inferior.

20. **The qualities they once claimed to admire about you suddenly become glaring faults.** At first, they appeal to

your deepest vanities and vulnerabilities, observing and mimicking exactly what they think you want to hear. But after you're hooked, they start to use these things against you. You spend more and more time trying to prove yourself worthy to the very same person who once said you were perfect.

21. **Cracks in their mask.** There are fleeting moments when the charming, cute, innocent persona is replaced by something else entirely. You see a side to them that never came out during the idealization phase, and it is a side that's cold, inconsiderate, and manipulative. You start to notice that their personality just doesn't add up—that the person you fell in love with doesn't actually seem to exist.

22. **Easily bored.** They are constantly surrounded by other people, stimulated and praised at all times. They can't tolerate being alone for an extended period of time. They become quickly uninterested by anything that doesn't directly impact them in a positive or thrilling way. At first, you might think they're exciting and worldly, and you feel inferior for preferring familiarity and consistency.

23. **Triangulation.** They surround themselves with former lovers, potential mates, and anyone else who provides them with added attention. This includes people that the psychopath may have previously denounced and declared you superior to. This makes you feel confused and creates the perception that the psychopath is in high demand at all times.

24. **Covert abuse.** From an early age, most of us were taught to identify physical mistreatment and blatant verbal insults, but with psychopaths, the abuse is not so obvious. You likely won't even understand that you were in an abusive relationship until long after it's over. Through personalized idealization and subtle devaluation, a psychopath can effectively erode the identity of *any* chosen target. From an outsider's perspective, you will appear to have "lost it," while the psychopath calmly walks away, completely unscathed.

25. **Pity plays and sympathy stories.** Their bad behavior always has sob-story roots. They claim to behave this way because of an abusive ex, an abusive parent, or an abusive cat. They say that all they've ever wanted is some peace and quiet. They say they hate drama—and yet there's more drama surrounding them than anyone you've ever known.

26. **The mean and sweet cycle.** Sometimes they shower you with attention, sometimes they ignore you, sometimes they criticize you. They treat you differently in public than they do behind closed doors. They could be talking about marriage one day and breaking up the next. You never know where you stand with them. As my morning-coffee friend Rydia wrote: "They put forth as little effort as possible and then step it up when you try to disengage."

27. **This person becomes your entire life.** You're spending more of your time with them and their friends, and less

time with your own support network. They're all you think and talk about anymore. You isolate yourself in order to make sure you're available for them. You cancel plans and eagerly wait by the phone for their next communication. For some reason, the relationship seems to involve a lot of sacrifices on your end, but very few on theirs.

28. **Arrogance.** Despite the humble, sweet image they presented in the early stages, you start to notice an unmistakable air of superiority about them. They talk down to you as if you are intellectually deficient and emotionally unstable. They have no shame when it comes to flaunting new targets after the breakup, ensuring that you see how happy they are without you.

29. **Backstabbing gossip that changes on a whim.** They plant little seeds of poison, whispering about everyone, idealizing them to their face, and then complaining about them behind their backs. You find yourself disliking or resenting people you've never even met. For some reason, you might even feel special for being the one he or she complains to. But once the relationship turns sour, they'll run back to everyone they once insulted to you, lamenting about how crazy you've become.

30. **Your feelings.** Your natural love and compassion has transformed into overwhelming panic and anxiety. You apologize and cry more than you ever have in your life. You barely sleep, and you wake up every morning feeling anx-

ious and unhinged. You have no idea what happened to your old relaxed, fun, easygoing self. After a run-in with a psychopath, you will feel insane, exhausted, drained, shocked, and empty. You tear apart your entire life—spending money, ending friendships, and searching for some sort of reason behind it all.

You will find that normal, loving people do not raise any of these flags. After an encounter with a psychopath, most survivors face the struggle of hypervigilance: Who can really be trusted? Your gauge will swing back and forth for a while, like a volatile pendulum. You will wonder if you've gone absolutely mad—wanting to believe the best in an old friend or a new date, but feeling sick to your stomach when you actually spend time with them because you're waiting for the manipulative behavior to start.

Developing your intuition is a personal process, but I would leave you with this: the world is mostly full of good people, and you don't want to miss out on that because you've been hurt. Spend some time getting in touch with your feelings. Keep tweaking until you find a comfortable balance between awareness and trust. Look within and understand why you felt the way you did when you were with your abusive partner and how you felt before you met them. You will discover that many old relationships may need revisiting. And as you begin to abandon toxic patterns, healthier ones will inevitably appear in their place.

To quote a longtime member and friend, Phoenix, you will stop asking "Do they like me?" and start asking "Do I like them?"

What Is Normal?

If your "soul mate" went from fascinated to bored in the blink of an eye, this is not normal. If you were called jealous and crazy by someone who actively cheated on you, this is not normal. If you were desperately waiting by your phone for texts they once initiated on a minute-by-minute basis, this is not normal. If all of their exes were "bipolar" or "madly in love" with them, this is not normal. Psychopaths are parasitic, emotionally stunted, and incapable of change. Once this individual is gone from your life, you will find that everything begins to make sense again. The chaos dissipates and your sanity returns. Things will be normal once again.

Beware the Vultures

You are taking the first steps to recover from a toxic relationship with a psychopath. That's great! The work you'll be doing will not only free you from the grasp of your abuser, but it will also enable you to reclaim yourself—the self that was trampled on, beaten down, and transformed into a shell of who you once were. I know it may be difficult to face some of the truths we'll be exploring, but it's also empowering, as you'll see how much you've survived, how strong you really are.

As you begin this work, I strongly encourage you to seek out a recovery professional or a healing community. You'll need the support and, at times, an encouraging reminder that you're on the right path.

I'd like to extend a special warning to those of you who are new to recovery. After psychopathic abuse, you're going to be extremely raw and vulnerable. As you start to put the pieces together, you'll feel devastated, miserable, and angry. It's overwhelming.

You're probably used to repressing your emotions and dealing with things on your own. But this time, everything is out in the open. You're dependent like a newborn child, seeking out someone—anyone—to understand what you're going through.

In general, it's important to be open with your emotions. But at your most insecure moments, you may unknowingly open the floodgates for more abuse.

It's no mystery that survivors seem to attract more pathological people like magnets. As you frantically share your story, you latch on to the quickest and most sympathetic ear—anyone who claims to understand you. The problem is, these people do not always have your best interests at heart.

Those willing to listen to your psychopathic story for hours on end are, unfortunately, not likely to be people who are truly invested in your recovery. They are most likely "vultures."

Vultures often seem exceptionally kind and warm at first. They want to fix you and absorb your problems. They are fascinated by your struggles. But sooner or later, you will find yourself lost in another nightmare. They begin drowning you in unsolicited advice. They need constant praise and attention. You are never allowed to disagree with them. They feed off drama and an insatiable need to be appreciated by others.

You will find that they lash out as you become happier. They perceive your progress as a threat to their control. They want to keep you in a perpetual state of dependency. They do not want you to seek help from anyone except them.

Whether these people are pathological or not, you don't need this toxic garbage after what you've been through.

I would strongly urge all survivors to avoid seeking out new friendships and relationships for at least a few months. You must get to the point where you no longer need—or want—to talk about your abuser anymore.

When you do need help, stick to professional therapy or recovery communities and services. These people know what you've been through, and you're going to find that all of them are willing to help—with no strings attached.

I understand the temptation to go out and meet new people. You're looking to start rebuilding your life. You want to surround yourself with kinder and more genuine friends.

And you will.

But real friends won't be acting as your therapist, and they definitely won't be rambling on about their ability to empathize and care. Their actions should speak louder than their words.

It takes a long time to start building healthier relationships. It takes breaking old habits, forming new ones, developing your intuition, and finally coming to understand what it is that you want from this world.

So be on the lookout for vultures. In the writing world, there's a universal rule called "show—don't tell." This rule also applies to people. If you encounter someone who's constantly telling you who they are, how much they want to help you, how they will make things right for you, take a step back and look at their actual behavior. Manipulative people are always "telling" because they have nothing good to show. Their inappropriate and dishonest actions never actually match up with their promising words, causing an overwhelming cognitive dissonance in the people who trust them.

You will find that decent, humble human beings aren't trying to tell you who they are and what they can do for you. They simply show it through consistent love and kindness. You never need to question them, because their intentions are always pure. Vultures, on the other hand, are really acting out of self-interest; they want to be praised and adored. In an argument, a "teller" will frequently remind you of how well they treat you, even after blatantly hurting you. A "show-er" will simply share their point of view without trying to twist the conversation in their favor. Avoid those who tell you how nice they are, how generous they are, how successful they are, how honest they are, and how important they are. Instead, search for the quiet ones who show these qualities every day through their actions.

The Constant

You know about psychopaths. You've got the red flags. So now the big question: Are you really involved with a psychopath?

Well, barring any major scientific advancements, you really can't know for certain whether or not someone has a conscience. In fact, I don't think there's any approach that will allow you to spot a psychopath with 100 percent confidence.

Fortunately, there's a different way to keep yourself safe. And this one involves looking within. It will work with anyone, anywhere, anytime. It's a question with answers—lots of them.

"How are you feeling today?"

Seriously, I'm asking you. Because most people might respond with a vague "fine" and follow up with a casual comment about their weekend, a promotion at work, or their favorite television show.

But what about you? Perhaps you're feeling empty? Broken? Hopeless? Maybe you woke up with that constant aching in your heart, eating away at your soul like a cancer. You spend the day trying to keep your thoughts free from painful topics—only to find that your mind keeps racing right back to them. Memories that once brought you so much joy now make you feel sick. You oscillate between anger and depression because you are unable to decide which one hurts less.

Those are answers.

So when you feel those things after a relationship, does it really matter if your ex was a psychopath, a sociopath, a narcissist, or a garden-variety jerk? The label doesn't make your feelings any more or less valid. Your feelings are absolutes. They will endure, no matter which word you settle upon.

And here's what you know from those feelings: someone uprooted your life, introducing a new kind of anxiety that you've never felt before. They've introduced you to a whole range of horrible emotions that make each day seem unbearable. During the relationship, you may have felt constantly on edge and unhinged, worried that any mistake could mark the end of your dream. Maybe you found yourself desperately comparing yourself to other people, trying to win back your rightful place by your partner's side.

So I ask you again, does it matter if they are a psychopath by definition?

You already have everything you need to know—from your own feelings. You felt horrible around them, right? So during the relationship, why wasn't that enough to confirm that they should have no place in your life?

Because you were groomed and idealized. You were tricked into falling in love—the strongest of all human bonds—so that your feelings could be more easily manipulated.

Toxic people condition us to ignore our intuition, and we must learn to trust it again. Instead of judging outwardly, we need to perceive inwardly. When we start focusing on our own feelings, this is where the healing begins. And if you are anything like me, we can agree on this simple truth: good people make you feel good and bad people make you feel bad.

Everything else falls into place from there.

Don't listen to the folks who say your feelings should be totally independent of the world around you. If you've got an open heart, that's impossible. As human beings, we have this incredible gift— the ability to make another person feel wonderful. With a word, a gesture, or a quiet smile. It's what makes the world beautiful. Some people would call this love.

But you experienced an abuser, someone who manipulated this gift in order to cause pain. And now you want to know how to avoid people like this so it'll never happen again. You're worried that you've become hypervigilant—untrusting of everyone and everything around you. You feel that you need a little something extra. Something beyond your intuition.

So this is where I'd like to introduce the idea of a Constant. Your Constant will comfort and protect you throughout this book, and for the rest of your life.

Think of someone you love. Someone who consistently inspires and never disappoints. It could be anyone—your mom, a close friend, your children, your cat, a deceased relative. Really, anyone. You might feel that you have no Constant. Of course you do; you can even dream one up. Imagine a higher power in your mind—one that brings peace to your heart. Colorful, glowing, and full of life. Embodying all of the qualities you admire most: empathy, compassion, kindness. A gentle spirit who will always keep you safe. And voilà, you have a Constant.

So now that you've got a Constant in mind (tangible or imagined), I have some questions. Does your Constant make you feel unhinged? Anxious? Jealous? Does your heart rise up into your throat when they speak to you? When you're away from your Constant, do you spend hours analyzing their behavior and defending yourself from hypothetical arguments?

Of course not.

So why is that? Why can one dismissive person make you doubt everything good going on in your life? What's the difference between your Constant and the people who make you feel like garbage?

If you can't answer these questions quite yet, you're not alone. And that's the beauty of it all. You do not need to understand why you don't like being around a person. You have a

Constant, and that's all you need to know for now. Self-respect comes later.

Your Constant is a private reminder that you are not crazy, even when it feels like you're taking on the entire world. With time, you will begin to filter out the people who make you feel bad. You realize that you do not need to put up with negativity when there is a Constant who brings out the best in you.

Once you become more comfortable with the idea, you'll be ready to ask the most important question of all: Shouldn't I feel this same kind of peace with everyone in my life?

Absolutely. So let's get started.

the manufactured soul mate

Perhaps most insidious of all the psychopath's evils: their relationship cycle, during which they gleefully and systematically wipe out the identity of an unsuspecting victim. Cold and calculated emotional rape.

Personalized Grooming

The psychopath trains you to become the perfect partner. In a matter of weeks, they take over your entire life, consuming your mind and body with unrivaled pleasure. Ultimately, you are to become their newest source of endless adoration and praise—but first, you must fall in love. Then your heart will be open to their every suggestion. There are three key components to this process: idealization, indirect persuasion, and testing the waters.

Idealization

The idealization phase in a psychopathic relationship will be unlike anything you've ever experienced. You will be swept off your feet, lost in a passionate fantasy with someone who excites you on every level: emotionally, spiritually, and sexually. They will be the first thing on your mind when you wake up in the morning, waiting for their cheerful, funny texts to start your day. You will quickly find yourself planning a future with them—forgetting about the dull realities of life. None of that matters anymore. They're the person you want to spend the rest of your life with.

While all of this is going on in your heart, their thoughts are occupied by something else entirely: "Good. It's working."

Psychopaths never truly feel the things they display. They're observing you, mirroring your every emotion, and pretending to ride this high with you.

Because the higher you rise, the lower you'll fall.

Idealization is the first step in the psychopath's grooming process. Also known as love-bombing, it quickly breaks down your guard, unlocks your heart, and modifies your brain chemicals to become addicted to the pleasure centers firing away. The excessive flattery and compliments play on your deepest vanities and insecurities—qualities you likely don't even know you possess.

They will feed you constant praise and attention through your phone, Facebook Timeline, and email inbox. Within a matter of weeks, the two of you will have your own set of inside jokes, pet names, and cute songs. Looking back, you'll see how insane the whole thing was. But when you're in the middle of it, you can't even imagine life without them.

So how did they do it?

Aside from gifts and poems, the psychopath uses a variety of brainwashing techniques to win you over. They will emphasize six major points during the idealize process:

1. We Have So Much in Common

We see the world the same way. We have the same sense of humor. We're both so empathetic, constantly helping out our friends and family members. We are perfect for each other.

The psychopath repeatedly drills these points home, oftentimes even going so far as to say: "We're practically the same person." During the grooming phase, psychopaths observe and mimic. They steal qualities from their victims, and almost seem to become a "better" version of their target's personality—co-opting all of the cheerful positives, without any of the burdensome emotions that come along with them. But this is all an act. These amplified, mirrored qualities are nothing more than a facade. Psychopaths don't truly feel or understand any of the things they imitate. They are able to offer a superficial and flattering copy of their victim's personality. Nothing more. None of the depth, compassion, and empathy that come along with being human. Like everything else they have to offer, their copycat personalities are hollow and empty.

The psychopath will spend most of the idealization phase listening to you and excitingly responding that he or she feels the same way as you do. You will eventually come to think that they're the only person you'll ever meet who's so similar to you. And you're right. Because it is flat-out impossible (and creepy) for two people to be identical in every way.

Normal people have differences. It's what makes life interesting. But psychopaths can skip this complication because they don't have an identity. They do not have a sense of self. They don't have life experiences that shape their needs, insecurities, and fantasies.

Instead, they steal yours. Like a chameleon, they will mimic every part of your personality to become your perfect match.

2. We Have the Same Hopes and Dreams

The psychopath will consume your present life, but they will also take over your future. In order to raise the stakes in the relationship, they will make many long-term promises. This ensures that you are highly invested in the relationship. After all, who wants to stick around for a romance that has no future?

The psychopath takes this a step further, quickly discussing major life events like marriage and moving in together. These are decisions that typically take years to arrive in a healthy relationship. But you don't need all that time. You already know you'll be spending the rest of your life with them. If you've always dreamed of a family and kids, they will fit that role perfectly. If you want to start a business, they will be your right-hand man or woman. If you're in an unhappy marriage, they will have a plan ready to replace your spouse. (What you might not notice until later is that these plans always seem to involve some sort of sacrifice on your end—never theirs.)

3. We Share the Same Insecurities

The psychopath will never actually mention your vulnerabilities, but they can sniff them out in a second. Then they will mirror your insecurities to drive up your sympathy—so that you attempt to heal their problems with the same care you might hope to receive yourself.

As an empathetic person, you are naturally drawn to offer comfort to people who are hurting or vulnerable. This inclination to comfort increases when you also recognize someone else's insecurities as your own. You see someone feeling inferior, and you believe that you know how to make them feel better.

The psychopath seems to genuinely adore all of your efforts. They compare you to their exes, idealizing you above everyone else. They praise your caring nature, which makes you want to do more for them. You feel that all of your efforts are appreciated, and you want to do even more to prove how much you care. You see their insecurities and perceive them as genuine, open, vulnerable, and sympathetic—someone you want to help. Psychopaths see insecurities in a very different way—as a tool for manipulation and control.

4. You Are Beautiful

The psychopath is obsessed with the way you look. You will never meet another human being who comments so frequently on your clothes, your hair, your skin, your pictures, or whatever other superficial quality they choose to focus on that day. At first, these words feel like compliments. They can't believe how beautiful you are—they don't even feel worthy of being your partner. They say they walk around the park and can't find a person more attractive than you (how this is a compliment, I'm not quite sure).

Going along with the idea of insecurities, you begin to return all of this flattery. You want to make sure they feel adequate—that they understand how attractive you think they are. And that's what they're aiming for. By showering you with compliments, they know they can expect the adoration to rebound shortly. Suddenly they become very comfortable sharing photos of themselves with you. Your relationship becomes an unending exchange of praise and approval.

You begin to place your self-esteem in their words, because they are so reliably positive. You can actually feel yourself glowing. Your body goes through changes as your confidence rises with their every word. You spend more and more time improving your appearance to keep them impressed.

5. I've Never Felt This Way in My Life

This is where the comparisons begin. They hold you in high regard, far above all of their other relationships. They explain—in detail—every one of the reasons you are better than their exes. They can't remember the last time they've been this happy.

You will constantly hear sweeping declarations like "I can't believe how lucky I am." Statements like these play on your innate desire to make others happy. They convince you that you're providing them with a special sort of joy, something that they cannot find in anyone else. This becomes a point of pride for you—knowing that you are the one they want, despite all of their other admirers.

The psychopath will refer to you as "perfect" and "flawless," which becomes an overwhelming source of cognitive dissonance when the words inevitably change to "crazy" and "jealous." As you work through these memories, remember that their compliments were always shallow and calculated. They use these tactics with everyone. For each target, the idealization phase will be different. However, one thing remains true throughout each relationship: they really have "never felt this way" in their life. Psychopaths do not actually feel the love and happiness that they so frequently proclaim. They oscillate between contempt, envy, and boredom. Nothing more.

6. We Are Soul Mates

Psychopaths love the idea of soul mates. It implies something different from love. It implies that there are higher powers at work. That you are meant to be together. It means that they consume your entire being—mind and body. It creates a psychic bond that lasts long after the relationship has ended.

Perhaps there is a small part in all of us that longs for a soul mate—the perfect person to complete our lives, someone with whom we can share everything, a lover and a best friend.

And there is nothing wrong with this. I cannot stress the point enough. Psychopaths will manipulate your dreams and fantasies, but that does not invalidate your dreams and fantasies and make them weaknesses.

After being discarded by a psychopath, many survivors denounce everything about their past life, raising a permanent guard to protect themselves from more abuse. Please don't do this.

If you believe in soul mates, you will find a real one. You will meet a man or woman who is full of gentle compassion and kindness. You will never question your heart because of them. Your love will blossom on its own, without all of the manufactured intensity. The psychopath was not your soul mate, and they never will be. To be your soul mate, they would—of course—need to have a soul.

After reading the above list, you may feel angry with yourself for falling for this duplicity. "How could I be so stupid?" you might ask. But please, don't beat yourself up. You weren't targeted because you were stupid. On the contrary, you were chosen because of so many good qualities you possess. A psychopath's perfect target is idealistic, forgiving, generous, and romantic. Most targets are very selective about their partners, often feeling lonely and frustrated by the dating scene. So when the psychopath comes along to mirror all of your greatest fantasies, you pour your entire heart and soul into the relationship. You'll invest everything you can—emotionally, financially, and physically. You quickly feel comfortable opening up because the psychopath grooms you to believe you've found "the one." This forms an immediate bond of trust and familiarity.

However, when the psychopath begins the devaluing process, you'll attempt to absorb all of the blame in the relationship, in order to restore the perfect memory you had of the person who once claimed to be your soul mate. This is why psychopathy awareness is so important. Without the missing puzzle piece, it is only logical to assume that this "soul mate" existed at some point, and might return again with enough love and care. But once we understand psychopathy, we come to realize that this person never existed at all. It was a mirror image—a carbon copy—of everything we wanted in a partner. When psychopaths lose this element of surprise, their pool of victims diminishes significantly.

Indirect Persuasion

After they've idealized you, they're ready to begin conditioning your behavior. Using indirect persuasion, psychopaths are able to make subtle suggestions that will ultimately be accepted by their victims. They maintain an illusion of innocence, since most people won't believe "they made me feel these things."

One method they use involves the way they offer compliments. They will insult their exes as a way to flatter their target, but what they are really doing is grooming their target. For instance, by saying "my ex always used to do this, but you never do that," they are *telling* you to behave a certain way. This is not a compliment—it's a warning that if you repeat any of the ex's alleged behavior, you'll be discarded as well. The ex likely didn't even do any of these things. It's just a way for the psychopath to indirectly tell you how they expect you to behave. Here are some of the most common examples:

- "My ex and I always fought. We never fight."
- "My ex always needed to talk on the phone. You're not needy or demanding."
- "My ex would always nag me about getting a job. You're so much more understanding."

Let me say it again: These are not compliments. They are expectations. The psychopath has come up with a checklist of human traits and emotions that bother them, and now they're planting the idea in your mind: don't express these things, or else.

Now, when you fight, you will try to end it as quickly and pleasantly as possible so you're not like their ex. When you haven't heard from them in three days, you won't call because you don't want to be like their ex. When they're sitting on their rear end, unemployed for six months, you won't say anything because you don't want to be like their ex.

Any deviation from this plan, and you will receive the silent treatment or a sharp comment about your changed behavior—a reminder that the idealization could end at any time.

This is why most survivors feel so much anger after the abuse has ended. You've been shoving aside your own intuition and needs in order to be "nice." You think you've been giving them some sort of special treatment that no one else can provide. And then suddenly they go running back to the very same people they used to complain about. Meanwhile, you've been repressing the urge to tell them to get a job, or call more often, or just be a good partner. You pushed all of that away because you thought it was the only way to stay with them, to stay on their good side.

Just remember, normal, empathetic people do not make such comparisons about the people they love. And they certainly don't keep a tally for everyone involved to see publicly. When you're truly in love, you don't need to convince yourself and others that this experience is better than all of your past experiences. Likewise, if you're falling out of love, you don't need to convince yourself and others that this experience is worse than all of your past experiences.

But psychopaths do this. Every single time. Because it's a strategically ambiguous way to influence your behavior.

No Support

Psychopaths provide shallow praise and flattery only in order to gain trust. When you actually need emotional support, they will typically offer an empty response—or they will completely ignore you. With time, this conditions you not to bother them with your feelings, even when you need a partner the most, especially during times of tragedy or illness. You will begin to notice that you are never allowed to express anything but positive praise for them. And even then, they will become bored soon enough and move on to the next target. Unable to empathize with pain and suffering, psychopaths cannot provide compassion during difficult times. This is why their "support" will always feel hollow and mechanical at best.

The "Crazy" Ex

Psychopaths talk about their exes a lot—more than any healthy individual with a new romantic partner should. After first making you feel like the only person in the world, they quickly try to evoke your pity by sharing stories about their nasty ex who's so very jealous of you and your passionate new relationship. Because these stories are completely invented, they can and absolutely will change on a whim. One day their ex is bipolar, the next day they're great friends, and then finally the ex is crazy and hysterical. And before long, you will become the "crazy ex" used to lure in a new victim.

But what do all of these labels really mean? What purpose do they serve?

"My Ex Is Bipolar"

Name-calling someone "bipolar" is like name-calling someone "diabetic." Bipolar disorder is a crippling illness with a specific set of symptoms that are a bit more complicated than "mood swings that I happen to dislike." Also called manic-depressive illness, it is characterized by unusual mood shifts, with reoccurring episodes of mania and depression. While bipolar disorder is real, how likely is it that their ex was bipolar? More likely, it is an insult they throw around to evoke your sympathy. It shouldn't be surprising, then, that when your relationship ends you'll likely carry this label as well.

If you suddenly became "bipolar" after a relationship with someone, and you've never been bipolar before, then you might want to think twice before accepting the diagnosis—especially if that diagnosis came from your ex.

The thing about "bipolar" is that it's actually a perfect label for the psychopath's ideal victim. If you're naturally cheerful and optimistic, these traits become your "mania." Then your valid reactions to your partner's abuse become the "depression." During the idealization phase, when the psychopath was charming and mirroring your entire personality, you were walking on sunshine. Life was amazing. But then they began criticizing you and cheating on you, so you became upset and cried. They gave you the silent treatment, all the while dangling new and former lovers in your face. Did this upset you? Excellent. Voilà, you're bipolar!

It horrifies me to think about the number of victims who falsely diagnose themselves based on volatile emotions that were intentionally provoked by someone else. Most survivors find that it takes one to two years for their moods to fully restabilize. Until that point, please be very reserved about deciding what's wrong with you.

Note: Millions of adults truly do suffer from bipolar disorder. If you're genuinely concerned about your mental health, please seek the opinion of a professional, not an ex-partner whose behavior drove you to a book called *Psychopath Free*.

"My Ex Is Crazy and Hysterical"

And it's definitely not worth thinking about how they came to be that way, right?

Seriously, though, let's think about it. This insult implies one of two things:

1. **Their ex was always crazy and hysterical, and for some reason, they still decided to date that person.** Seems unhealthy, no?

2. **Something changed during the relationship to make the ex that way.** What exactly could it be? Did they just snap one day, for absolutely no reason at all? Or did it maybe have something to do with the constant triangulation, lying, manipulating, and criticizing? If someone tells you

how "crazy" their ex is, you should take a step back and *really* rethink that one.

This characterization serves another purpose; it informs you about what is considered "acceptable" behavior. "Crazy" and "hysterical" are words of invalidation, minimization, and dismissal. They imply that the reactions this person displayed were over-the-top. You will be wary of acting this way, too. This strategy encourages you to stop reacting, and thereby to stop standing up for yourself. By making you question your own sanity, the psychopath is able to take the spotlight away from their own abusive behavior.

"My Ex Is Bitter"

What the heck? Seriously, what does this even mean? It's like punching someone in the face and then saying "you're bitter." Well, yeah, that person is bitter because you punched them in the face. Does saying "you're bitter" somehow make the bitterness inappropriate?

Again, it's about minimization and dismissal. After their abusive behavior, lying, and mind games, the psychopath expects their victim to simply shut up or grovel. That's it. Any signs of anger or disbelief are equated with bitterness. The psychopath will then commiserate with their new partner about their ex being childish and holding grudges, neglecting to mention all of the details that suggest why that person might be bitter in the first place.

"My Ex Is Jealous of Us and Still in Love with Me"

First of all, who brags about something like this? It's so off-putting, and even if it's true, this sort of pigheaded arrogance should be avoided in any sort of romantic endeavor.

Digging deeper, we should also examine *why* this person is jealous and still in love with them. Psychopaths typically flaunt their new victims for the whole world to see mere days after their previous relationship ended. You know what that does? Gasp, it creates jealousy.

Psychopaths manufacture toxic, desperate love. And the thing about this sort of idealized and then devalued passion is that it's long-lasting and obsessive. Psychopaths groom others to spend every waking moment thinking about them, and then they tear it all away without a moment's notice. Because psychopaths are eternally bored and incapable of human bonding, this transition is quite easy for them. But to a normal, healthy individual, it's devastating. You send desperate texts in an attempt to fix everything, unaware that they're using these frantic communications as "proof" of your insanity to garner sympathy from their next victim. It leaves you with a broken heart, crippling insecurities, a need to defend yourself, feelings of inferiority, and a million unanswered questions. This is why it takes so long to get over a psychopath.

These claims of jealousy also serve to make their new target feel special—as if they are the chosen one among the psychopath's many admirers. The psychopath will gladly string obedient exes along to make themselves seem in high demand at all times.

"But My Ex Really Was Awful!"

Everyone has horror stories about their exes. That's perfectly normal. What's not normal is when an ex's name comes up so frequently in a new relationship that you begin to feel like they're actually a part of your relationship. It's also not normal to trash an ex and then hang out with them on a daily basis. Trust your intuition, and remember that psychopaths always use exes as tools for manipulation and persuasion.

The bottom line is this: anyone who speaks so regularly and so negatively about their ex is—at best—not at all ready for a romantic relationship. But at worst, this person is manipulating your every thought, pitting you against people you've never even met. And you can be assured that they'll soon be speaking the exact same way about you to every other pawn in their never-ending game of chess.

Testing the Waters

Once they have you programmed, psychopaths will begin experimenting with their newfound control to see how far they can push you. A useful victim will not talk back, and they certainly won't defend themselves if the situation calls for it. If the idealization phase worked as planned, you should be more invested in maintaining the passion than standing up for yourself.

During this period, you will see tiny glimpses of the psychopath's darker side. They may teasingly call you a "whore" in the bedroom to see how you react. If you're married to someone else, they might casually joke about your spouse's ignorance about the whole situation. They will begin making subtle digs about your intelligence, abilities, and dreams.

These are all tests, and unfortunately if you're reading this book, it means you passed them. If you react in a negative way, the psychopath will assure you that they were obviously joking. As they test the waters, you will begin to feel more and more oversensitive. You've always considered yourself to be an exceptionally easygoing person, but now you're questioning that. You stop mentioning your concerns, optimistically hoping to keep things perfect.

They use these subtle digs in combination with flattery, ensuring that the addictive brain chemicals continue to fire even when you're feeling upset. This trick slowly trains your mind to ignore your intuition, in favor of the high you feel when you're with them.

If you look back at the early stages of your relationship, you will likely remember small warning signs that you tried to ignore—signs that just didn't fit in with the whole "nice person" act. Maybe they bragged a little bit too much about how much their ex still wants them. Or perhaps they "forgot" to call when they promised they would, contacting you hours later than planned. They probably stopped paying for dates, letting you pick up the tab. So what did you do? You brushed it all aside. You forgave them quickly and moved forward because you were determined to be different—the partner who could keep them happy and absorb anything, no matter the cost.

And that's when the grooming is complete.

Identity Erosion

The psychopath strips you of your dignity by taking back everything they once pretended to feel during the idealization period. They make a mockery of your dreams, subtly suggesting that you may not be the one for them after all—but nonetheless stringing you along for the added attention. After grooming you to be dependent and compliant, they use this power to manufacture desperation and desire. In a whirlwind of overwhelming emotions, your fantasy gradually shifts into an inconceivable nightmare.

Destroying Your Boundaries

Emotional abusers condition their victims to feel ashamed, inadequate, and unstable. This is because they are cowards, incapable of healthy relationships with strong and self-respecting individuals. Oftentimes, they choose targets who are unusually successful and idealistic, because these people have more to lose. But abusers cannot control someone with such qualities, and so they break down the target's self-esteem through belittling, teasing, and manufactured jealousy. The target may have perfectionist tendencies, striving to meet the abuser's impossible standards. This results in a strange dynamic where the abuser is idealized, despite being lazy, dishonest, and unfaithful, while the victim is devalued, despite putting more effort into this relationship than ever before.

Like sandpaper, the psychopath will wear away at your self-esteem through a calculated "mean and sweet" cycle. Slowly, your standards will fall so low that you become grateful for utterly mediocre treatment. Like a frog in boiling water, you won't even realize what's happened until it's far too late. Your friends and family will wonder what happened to the man or woman who used to be so strong and energetic. You will frantically excuse your partner's behavior, unable to acknowledge the painful truth behind your relationship: something has changed.

You spend hours waiting by the phone, hoping for that morning text message or a promised phone call. You cancel your plans for the day just to make sure you'll be available for them. You begin to initiate contact more often, brushing aside the nagging sensation that they don't want to talk with you—that they're simply "putting up" with you. You find yourself filling their Facebook wall with compliments and cute jokes, trying to reestablish the perfect dream from the beginning of your relationship. But their responses now feel hollow at best.

You invent romantic stories and exaggerate their positive aspects to anyone who will listen. By convincing others that they are a wonderful person, you can continue to live the lie yourself. Throughout the worst of the relationship, your friends and family will likely know them as the "perfect" partner you described. After the relationship ends, it will be confusing and awkward to explain what really happened. Your stories will seem implausible, and your friends will wonder why you didn't speak up sooner. They will not understand that you didn't even know you were in an abusive relationship.

While you're struggling with all of this unexpected anxiety, the psychopath is able to push your boundaries even further. You're in a vulnerable place now, because you're willing to put up with mostly anything—so long as they're paying attention to you.

Their opinions about your appearance become much more critical than before. Suddenly they begin to notice every little part of your body, commenting freely on your supposed inadequacies. You may even develop an eating disorder, failing to take care of yourself in an effort to keep them interested. Psychopaths are fascinated by body-image issues, and will reward your unhealthy habits with the occasional compliment to keep you striving for perfection. Since your self-worth is invested entirely in their os-cillating opinions, your moods will become unstable and volatile.

They will also begin to humiliate you in front of friends—no longer limited to belittling you behind closed doors. But it will always be done under a guise of humorous intention. You will be hurt to see that others seem to take your partner's side and laugh, despite the way they're making you feel. A psychopath doesn't care when they take a joke too far, and they will dismiss any concerns you might have, accusing you of being hypersensitive. You begin to go along with it, playing the role of a crazy, unintelligent partner whose only purpose is to entertain your lover. With time, you will come to believe this facade.

All the while, they will sprinkle intermittent reminders of the idealization phase. If you reach a breaking point, they will always be ready to swoop back in with promises of unlimited love and affection. Although they will never take the blame for their behavior, these superficial distractions will be enough to convince you that they're still the person you fell in love with. And nothing else matters.

Manufactured Emotions

During a relationship with a psychopath, you are likely to experience a range of emotions that you've never felt before: extreme jealousy, neediness, rage, anxiety, and paranoia. After every outburst, you constantly think to yourself, "If only I hadn't behaved that way, then maybe they'd be happier with me."

Think again.

Those were not your emotions. I repeat: those were not your emotions. They were carefully manufactured by the psychopath in order to make you question your own good nature. Victims are often prone to believe that they can understand, forgive, and absorb all of the problems in a relationship. Essentially, they checkmate themselves by constantly trying to rationalize the abuser's completely irrational behavior.

The Serial Provoker

Serial provokers are experts at seeking out flexible, easy-going people. They exploit this quality by constantly provoking their target with covert jabs, minimization, veiled humor, and patronizing. The target will attempt to avoid conflict by remaining pleasant, choosing to forgive and excuse this behavior in favor of maintaining harmony. But the serial provoker will continue to aggravate the target until they finally snap. Once this occurs, the provoker will sit back, feign surprise, and marvel at how passive-aggressive, angry, and volatile the target is. The target will immediately feel bad, apologize, and absorb the blame. They are essentially shamed for rightfully losing their patience and behaving the way the serial provoker behaves every single day. The difference is, the target feels remorse—the serial provoker does not. The target is expected to remain calm and peaceful no matter what, while the serial provoker feels entitled to do whatever they please.

For example, you probably didn't consider yourself to be a jealous person before you met the psychopath. You might have even taken pride in being remarkably relaxed and open-minded. The psychopath recognizes this and seeks to exploit it. During the grooming phase, they draw you in by flattering you about those traits—they just can't believe how perfect you are. The two of you never fight. There's never any drama. You're so easygoing compared to their crazy, evil ex.

But behind the scenes, something else is going on. Psychopaths become bored very easily, and the idealization is only fun until they have you hooked. Once that happens, these strengths of yours become vulnerabilities that they use against you. They begin to inject as much drama into the relationship as they possibly can, throwing you into impossible situations and then judging you for reacting to them.

Most people would agree that jealousy is toxic in a relationship. But there's a huge difference between true jealousy and the psychopath's manufactured jealousy.

Take the following two (exaggerated) conversations:

CASE 1:

> BOYFRIEND: Hey, my old high school friend is coming into town if you'd like to meet her.
>
> GIRLFRIEND: No! Why do you need other female friends? You have me.

In this case, the girlfriend truly seems to have some jealousy issues that need to be addressed. Assuming the boyfriend hasn't abused her in the past, this is an inappropriate display of jealousy.

CASE 2:

> BOYFRIEND: My ex is coming into town. You know, the crazy abusive one who's still completely obsessed with me.
>
> GIRLFRIEND: Oh, I'm sorry to hear that!

BOYFRIEND: We're probably going to meet up later for drinks. She always hits on me when she drinks.

GIRLFRIEND: I'm confused. Could we talk about this in person?

BOYFRIEND: You have a problem with it?

GIRLFRIEND: Nope! No problem. I guess I was just a little confused since you said she abused you. But I hope things go well! It's nice when exes are able to be friends.

BOYFRIEND: Wow, you're so jealous sometimes.

GIRLFRIEND: I'm sorry. I'm not trying to be jealous. I was just confused at first.

BOYFRIEND: Your jealousy is ruining our relationship and creating so much unnecessary drama.

GIRLFRIEND: I'm sorry! We don't have to talk about it in person. I really didn't mean to come across that way.

BOYFRIEND: It's fine, I forgive you. We'll just have to work through your jealousy issues.

In this case, the psychopath did three things:

1. Put his girlfriend in an impossible situation that would make any human being jealous, especially after talking about how much his ex loves him.

2. Accused her of being jealous, even though she tried to respond reasonably.

3. Played "good cop" by offering to forgive her for a problem that he created in the first place. This places him in his favorite role of teacher vs. student.

The longer this abuse occurs, the more she'll begin to wonder if she actually has a jealousy problem.

And it's not just limited to jealousy. Perhaps you began to feel needy and clingy during the relationship with the psychopath. Again, it's all manufactured. Who was the one responsible for initiating constant conversation and attention in the first place? It was them. Once they're bored, they will start to lash out at you for trying to continue practices that they initiated.

Again, most people would agree that neediness is toxic in a relationship. But there's a huge difference between true neediness and the psychopath's manufactured neediness.

CASE 1:

GIRLFRIEND: Hey, I won't be around tonight because my grandmother wants to get dinner. Sorry!

BOYFRIEND: Oh my God, I haven't seen you in three hours. This is getting ridiculous. You better text me the entire time.

In this case, the boyfriend truly seems to have some neediness issues that need to be addressed. Assuming the girlfriend hasn't abused him in the past, this is an inappropriate display of neediness.

CASE 2:

BOYFRIEND: Hi, I haven't heard from you in three days. Just want to make sure you're doing okay.

GIRLFRIEND: God, I have a life outside of you, you know.

BOYFRIEND: I know, I was just sort of confused because I'm used to hearing from you each morning.

GIRLFRIEND: You're so needy. I have important things to do and I can't just drop everything to text you.

BOYFRIEND: I'm sorry, I didn't mean to sound needy. It was the first text I've sent in three days.

GIRLFRIEND: I can't deal with this. I've never met someone so needy in my life.

BOYFRIEND: I'm really sorry! I won't bother you again.

GIRLFRIEND: It's fine. I forgive you. We'll just have to work through your neediness issues.

Once again, the psychopath did three things:

1. Put her boyfriend in an impossible situation that would make any human being needy, especially after the constant attention in the idealization phase.

2. Accused him of being needy, even though he tried to respond reasonably.

3. Played "good cop" by offering to forgive him for a problem that she created in the first place. This places her in her favorite role of teacher vs. student.

The longer this abuse occurs, the more he'll begin to wonder if he's actually a needy person.

I could go on like this for paranoia, anger, hysteria—and every other nasty emotion you may have felt in your toxic relationship. When you're in the grip of these emotions, it is natural to wonder what's wrong with you. You might even think you're going crazy. Well, psychopaths want you to believe you're crazy because it makes you seem more unstable to the rest of the world. But you'll find that once they're gone from your life, everything starts to make sense again. If you went from normal to "crazy" to normal again, that's not crazy. That's someone provoking you.

You must understand that in loving, healthy relationships, no one would ever put you in these situations in the first place. Your boundaries were put to the test, and you did the absolute best you could, given the circumstances. In the future, you should never allow someone to tell you who you are or how you feel.

Word Salad

When they're feeling threatened or bored, the psychopath will often use what's called word salad in an attempt to keep your mind occupied. Basically, it's a conversation from hell. They aren't actually saying anything at all; they're just talking at you. Before you can even respond to one outrageous statement, they're already on to the next. You'll be left with your head spinning. Study the warning signs, and disengage before any damage can be done:

1. Circular Conversations

You'll think you worked something out, only to begin discussing it again in two minutes. And it's as if you never even said a word the first time around. They'll begin reciting all of the same tired garbage, ignoring any legitimate arguments you may have provided moments ago. If something is going to be resolved, it will be on their terms. With psychopaths, the same issues will come up over and over again: Why are they so friendly with their ex again? Why are they suddenly not paying any attention to you? Why do they sound so eager to get off the phone? And every time you bring up these issues, it's as if you never even had the argument in the past. You get sucked back in, only to feel crazy and high maintenance when they decide, "I'm sick of always arguing about this." It's a merry-go-round.

2. Bringing Up Your Past Wrongdoings and Ignoring Their Own

If you point out something nasty they're doing—like ignoring you or cheating—they'll mention something totally unrelated from the past that you've done wrong. Did you used to drink too much? Well then, their cheating isn't really all that bad compared to your drinking problem. Were you late to your first date two years ago? Well then, you can't complain about them ignoring you for three days straight. And God forbid you bring up any of their wrongdoings. Then you are a bitter lunatic with a list of grievances.

3. Condescending and Patronizing Tone

Throughout the entire conversation they will have this calm, cool demeanor. It's almost as if they're mocking you, gauging your reactions to see how much further they can push. When you finally react emotionally, that's when they'll tell you to calm down, raise their eyebrows, smirk, or feign disappointment. The whole point of word salad is to make you unhinged, and thereby give them the upper hand. Because remember, conversations are competitions—just like anything else with a psychopath.

4. Accusing You of Doing Things That They Themselves Are Doing

In heated arguments, psychopaths have no shame. They will begin labeling you with their own horrible qualities. It goes beyond projection, because most people project unknowingly. Psychopaths know they are smearing you with their own flaws, and they are seeking a reaction. After all, how can you not react to such blatant hypocrisy?

5. Multiple Personas

Through the course of a word-salad conversation, you're likely to experience a variety of their personalities. It's sort of like good cop, bad cop, demented cop, stalker cop, scary cop, baby cop. If you're pulling away, sick of their abuse and lies, they will evoke a glimpse of the idealization phase. A little torture to lure you back in with empty promises. If that doesn't work, suddenly they'll start insulting the things they once idealized. You'll be left wondering who you're even talking to, because their personas are imploding as they struggle to regain control. Our beloved administrator, Victoria, summed this up perfectly: "The devil itself was unleashed in a desperate fit of fury after being recognized:

twisting, turning, writhing, spewing, flattering, sparkling, vomiting."

6. The Eternal Victim

Somehow, their cheating and lying will always lead back to a conversation about their abusive past or a crazy ex. You will end up feeling bad for them, even when they've done something horribly wrong. You will use it as an opportunity to bond with them over their supposed complex feelings. And once they've successfully diverted your attention, everything will go back to the way it was. No bonding or deep spiritual connection whatsoever. Psychopaths cry "abuse"—but in the end, you are the only one being abused.

7. You Begin Explaining Basic Human Emotions

You find yourself explaining things like "empathy" and "feelings" and "being nice." Normal adults do not need to be taught the golden rules from kindergarten. You are not the first person who has attempted to see the good in them, and you will not be the last. You think to yourself, "If they can just understand why I'm hurt, then they'll stop doing it." But they won't. They wouldn't have hurt you in the first place if they were a decent human being. The worst part is, they pretended to be decent when you first met—sucking you in with this sweet, caring persona. They know how to be kind and good, but they find it boring.

8. Excuses

Everyone messes up every now and then, but the psychopath recites excuses more often than they actually follow through with promises. Their actions never match up with their words. You are disappointed so frequently that you feel relieved when they do something halfway decent—they condition you to become grateful for mediocre treatment.

9. "What in the World Just Happened?"

These conversations leave you drained. You will be left with an actual headache. You will spend hours, even days, obsessing over the argument. You'll feel as if you exhausted all of your emotional energy to accomplish absolutely nothing. You will have a million preplanned arguments in your head, ready to respond to all the unaddressed points that you couldn't keep up with. You will feel the need to defend yourself. You'll try to come up with a diplomatic solution that evenly distributes the blame, and therefore gives you both a chance to apologize and make up. But in the end, you'll find that you're the only one apologizing.

Gaslighting and Projection

Gaslighting is when the psychopath intentionally distorts reality—often with trivial lies and wrongdoings—to bring about a reaction and then deny that it ever took place. Like most victims, you are

Enemy Number One

Psychopaths carefully select targets and copy their personalities in order to create an immediate bond of trust and familiarity. But because they are only acting, they cannot play the role perfectly forever. So inevitably, their targets begin to notice small cracks in the mask—uncanny, inexplicable moments that simply don't seem to match up with the person they're pretending to be. Any target who dares point out these inconsistencies instantly becomes enemy number one. Instead of admitting fault and deceit, the psychopath will attempt to drive the target insane. Through mind games, triangulation, gaslighting, and silence, they innocently encourage the target to self-destruct. Most targets don't even know they're dealing with a pathological personality at the time. They might only have gently observed that "something feels different between us." But to a psychopath, this is the greatest insult of all—a challenge to their credibility as a normal, healthy human being. And so they must smear the target as "crazy" before quickly moving along to another victim who will better appreciate their world of lies.

probably exceptionally easygoing and will hold off on reacting for as long as possible. But inevitably, you're going to feel frustrated enough to finally speak up, and that's when the psychopath will either rewrite history or reject that the incident ever even occurred. You may start to doubt your own sanity as the psychopath slowly erodes your grasp on reality.

Gaslighting isn't usually blatant abuse. It could be as simple as them saying they're going to do one thing, and then doing something entirely different. For example, they may tell you they're on their way to the gym, but then they go to a restaurant with friends instead. What's the point of a lie like that? Why not just tell you they're going out to dinner?

Earlier on in the relationship, you might have innocently asked what happened to their gym plans and they would inevitably start to make up strange, pointless excuses. But as the abuse worsens, they'll likely deny that they ever even said they were going to the gym. You'll find yourself disagreeing with them and repeating the entire conversation, only to discover how petty you sound and how much you're annoying your partner.

And that's the thing about conversations that come from gaslighting: they *do* sound petty. Who wants to argue about gym plans turning into a dinner out on the town? Who cares? In any normal relationship, you wouldn't even bat an eye. But with psychopaths, these needless lies happen on a regular basis, and you find that you're always getting sucked into ridiculous, pointless conversations that make you seem like an obsessed detective.

Speaking of detectives, if you present evidence of the truth—like a text message or an email—the psychopath will punish you with the silent treatment and turn the entire conversation around on you for being paranoid and crazy. You slowly learn that you're becoming a nuisance and that open communication is unofficially prohibited in your relationship.

The Black Hole

Psychopaths always see themselves as victims, no matter how horribly they've treated someone else. Nothing is ever their fault—they've always been wronged in one way or another. To them, the problem is not their lying, cheating, stealing, and abuse. The problem is that you started to notice all of those things. Why couldn't you just remain happy with the idealization phase? How dare you betray them by standing up for yourself? Encounters with these people are like drowning in a black hole, because no matter how much they hurt you, it'll still be your fault.

Our invaluable administrator, Smitten Kitten, explains this mind-boggling process clearly and coherently:

"Psychopaths project and blame you for their own behavior. They accuse you of being negative when they are the most negative people in the world. They gaslight you into believing that your normal reactions to their abuse are the problem—not the abuse itself. When you feel angry and hurt because of their silent treatment, broken promises, lying, or cheating, there is something wrong with you. When you call them out on their dishonest behavior, you're the abnormal one who is too sensitive, too critical, and always focusing on the negative.

"This is all part of the brainwashing process. Acting inappropriately, unacceptably, downright abusively—and then trying to turn it around to make it your fault. They intentionally cause pain you don't deserve, all the while denying they've done anything to begin with. And on top of that, they try to make it your fault—so that you blame yourself for something that supposedly didn't even happen.

"Yes, reread that. That's how illogical it is.

"It's their parting 'gift' to dump all of the blame on you for the looming failure of the relationship. Problem is, it never had a chance to begin with.

"If only you had maintained the glowing optimism and naïveté you felt during the love-bombing stage—throughout all of their subsequent lies and abuse. Then everything would have been fine. If only you hadn't questioned the contradictions and lies you recalled from letters that they later denied sending. Yes, if only you had stayed compliant and quiet, in spite of the overwhelming evidence staring you in the face—evidence they planted, just to test you. Then it would all be fine.

"But even then, they would become bored and disappointed that you hadn't caught on or challenged them. So they'd invent something to accuse you of, in order to justify their abuse and create drama. No matter what you do, it's always a lose-lose situation with a psychopath. They want you to believe you're the loser when really, it's them."

Sexual Manipulation

Sex with the psychopath seemed perfect at first. They knew exactly where to touch you, what to say, and when to do the right things. You were perfectly compatible in the bedroom, right?

Well, sort of.

Like everything else, the psychopath also mirrored your deepest sexual desires. That's why it felt so incredibly passionate and flawless when you were together—and that's why it feels like rape during the identity erosion. Because the psychopath does not, in fact, share your most intimate fantasies. Instead, they've been observing and tailoring their behavior to match yours. It's shocking when you realize this, because you come to understand that they never felt the emotional and spiritual pleasure that you felt. While you were at your most vulnerable, they were simply watching and learning.

You find yourself in a desperate situation, needing their sexual approval and flattery to feel attractive. They use this to control you. They pull away in order to make you seem desperate, needy, and slutty. In the idealization phase, they couldn't get enough of you. But once they have you hooked, they begin to play mind games. They withhold sex, redefining it as a privilege that they hold the key to.

When you're lying next to them in bed, you can practically feel them waiting for you to make the next move. They're ready to mock you—to make you feel unnatural and sex-crazed. They will laugh at you, insulting you with jokes that aren't even remotely funny. The passionate sex you remember has been replaced by a game. A competition.

They will make you feel ugly by announcing that their sex drive is lower than ever—that they haven't even had sexual thoughts in weeks. The implication is clear: they haven't thought about you in weeks.

And then, when the triangulation begins, you find it impossible to believe that they could have such a great sex life with anyone else. How could they? You seemed like soul mates when you made love. They liked all of the same things as you. But remember, it was manufactured. If you loved something in the bedroom, the psychopath quickly picked up on that in the grooming phase. They'll pick up on something else entirely for their next victim.

You unknowingly formed a bond with a con artist. Your consent was based on a lie. So many survivors blame themselves because they couldn't get past the sexual addiction, keeping them bonded to their abuser. But it's not your fault. You were tricked into feeling an overwhelmingly strong attachment during the grooming phase. And then they manipulated that—toying with the toxic addiction firing through your body.

You will reclaim your sexual freedom—I promise. We have an open and honest dialogue about sex at PsychopathFree.com. It is a hugely important part of the psychopathic relationship cycle, and more importantly, it plays an essential role in your own healing process. Recovery is a joint effort of the mind and body.

The Transitional Target

This section comes directly from a conversation I had with a dear friend, so it may feel a bit personal at times. I've done my best to edit it to apply to a broader audience. It's a special note for anyone who felt unusually disposable compared to the psychopath's other targets.

Psychopaths are always on the prowl for their next target but as the psychopath transitions from one "stable" relationship to the next, they need something (someone) to fill the void in between: a temporary target to dispose of as soon as they find something else. If you are selected as a transitional target, you may find your treatment a bit different from what I've already described. Although the psychopath likely doesn't even have the next target scouted out yet, they already know they're not staying with you so they want to move things along quickly. Because of this, you tend to get ripped out of the idealize phase much faster than most. Additionally, the idealize phase is lazy: no money, no actions, no special treatment. Just words. You were showered with a lot of words, which sucked you in, because you wanted to believe the words so badly. But, as you're starting to see, their actions never match up with their words.

But to you, the relationship means everything—it's attention and appreciation you've never experienced before. It appeals to your deepest dreams of making someone else happy, after all of their alleged pain and sadness. It seems like they know you so well. You finally found a soul mate after so much loneliness and frustration.

Unfortunately, none of this is true. To the psychopath, you are merely a diversion. Psychopaths are especially indifferent with transitional targets, not really caring one way or another—leaving you with the feeling that they're being insensitive. You tend to fill in their abuse with your own love, in hopes that you can restore the brief idealize phase. Targets often experience cognitive dissonance, trying to project their own reasoning onto an unreasonable person. But the psychopath's behavior is neither accidental nor unintentional.

And then comes the most heartbreaking moment: they discard you and go running off with another person whom they suddenly seem ready to settle down with. They move in together, post pictures, pay for things, and live the life you always dreamed of. It's the ultimate insult when you were not given any of that special treatment. Basically, as soon as they got their quick fix of power and control over you, they felt re-energized and ready to scout out their next great adventure.

Statistically, most victims in an abusive relationship with a psychopath return to their abusers seven times before they finally realize the treatment is unacceptable and leave for good. Not so, for the transitional target. Here's how the two types of relationships play out:

Typical relationship with a psychopath:

Idealize, devalue, idealize, devalue, idealize, devalue (repeat)
→ *Finally a breaking point*

This is what transitional targets get:

Mediocre idealize phase with huge promises that make you feel amazing → *Sudden discard out of nowhere.*

This leaves the transitional target with zero closure because you can't even look back at the cycle of violence that exists for most people. Not that you would want to by any means, but you're basically just left in limbo after the abandonment, from such a ridiculous high to a devastating low, with no time or perspective to realize what just happened. It's emotional torture. You are left only with an intense love and a horrible discard.

Psychopaths use their mind games on every target—it's always the same. The difference is, transitional targets never experience that "full" idealize phase, with some time and stability for things to blow up. This is because the psychopath never intended for the transitional target to become a stable part of their life to begin with. You were perfect for what they wanted at the time: attention and admiration.

But they also recognized that you were emotionally intelligent and uniquely perceptive. The fact that you're reading this book is not some sort of accident—you're a truth seeker, determined to find out what just happened to you.

Psychopaths settle for targets who don't truly see their nasty behavior. If you're reading this now, that means the psychopath could never settle for you, because over the course of months, years, or decades, you saw through the facade. They need someone who won't catch on. Ever.

So yes, on one hand, the eventual long-term victim is useful, because they won't call out the psychopath's lying and cheating. But on the other hand, the psychopath silently resents these people for not seeing through their facade. Strange, right? They pretend to give off this perfect, happy image with their "settlement," but they much prefer the thrill of someone more empathetic— someone who truly feels the torture of their mind games. But the psychopath can rarely have one of these people permanently, so instead he or she uses them during transition periods, like a quick high before the settlement. (Every once in a while, though, they will end up spending years with a highly empathetic person. I know several of these people from the forum. They are usually locked into a psychopathic relationship because they have children with the psychopath. These dynamics often seem to result in horrific discards.)

Many survivors tell stories of love-bombing that lacked the actual courtship seen with the psychopath's next target or previous ex. You never got to spend as much time with them as the others, right? Instead, you experienced a much shorter fling, cut off abruptly in the middle of the idealize phase with some unbelievably vicious identity erosion. And then suddenly they've settled down with another partner, leaving you wondering how they're able to spend years with that person, when they could barely handle a few months with you.

And that's the point—psychopaths typically can't last long with empathetic people (except for cases with children and long-term manipulation), because you tend to absorb their poison. Yes, they get the high of sweeping you off your feet and making you a perfect servant to their mind games. But the downside is, eventually you subconsciously spit that poison right back in their face. You don't want to ruin the idealize phase, but you find yourself unable to stop pointing out their lies and changed behavior.

Transitional targets and truth-seeking targets figured them out, all the way down to their nasty core. Psychopaths would never admit it, but they'll always have a bitter respect for people who can see them for what they really are. And at the same time, they'll also strongly resent those who can't—even though that's all they can get in the long run. This is why they always lose and reinvent the rules of the game, to convince themselves that their choice is correct.

But the fact is, psychopaths settle. They always do. And that's why they needed to destroy you before settling: to convince themselves that they're not losing anything special. So why not make you self-destruct—even hurt yourself? Perfect, the nagging doubts are finally gone.

And from your perspective, this is why you're left so resentful and angry. You did so much, encouraged by their fake appreciation that kept you going. At the very least, why couldn't they be a jerk from the start so you'd know not to waste your time and emotions? Instead, they used words and promises to brainwash you into giving, giving, and more giving. So when they not only don't appreciate it—but actually destroy you—you're left feeling broken and empty. And then you see them running off with someone else, paying for things, settling down a bit . . . It makes you think "Hey, maybe they are capable of a relationship after all. Maybe the problem was me."

No, the problem was not you. And it never will be.

Putting You on the Defensive

If you're dealing with a psychopath, it's a given that they will make unfounded accusations about you at some point—especially if you're starting to put together the red flags in their behavior. These insults have a very specific purpose: to put you on the defensive.

Why?

It's actually a lot simpler than you might think. People who defend themselves seem guilty by default. Whether or not they're guilty doesn't matter. Once they start to defend themselves, opinions and assumptions are made. Is it unfair? You bet. But it's how people often react. We've seen lives destroyed because of this phenomenon—a man falsely accused of rape will continue to be thought of as a rapist, even after he's been proven innocent. The truth doesn't matter. No one trusts him anymore.

So the psychopath says all sorts of ridiculous things, and you're suddenly defending yourself from accusations you've never even dreamed of. How could you not? Your name is being smeared—if not to others, then to the partner who supposedly loves you. So you get caught up in trying to prove them wrong, and that's where the calculated self-destruction begins.

The psychopath can sit back, relax, and enjoy the show. They can calmly point to the hysterical victim and say, "Jeez, that poor, crazy person . . ." Essentially, they provoke your anger, and then calmly use it to prove their own point.

You may try to expose their lies: "They're the liar, here's the proof!" or "They cheated on me, here's the proof!" or "They've done the same thing with ten other partners, here's the proof!" The problem is, nobody cares about the proof. They just see you desperately trying to defend yourself, and because you're defending yourself, you seem like the guilty one.

Here's the most important thing to remember: defending yourself will only make things worse. Sometimes less is more, and this is one of those times. You think you have a perfect response to their ridiculous defamation? Yes, the psychopath is counting on that. In fact, they've carefully crafted their insults to make sure of it. They attack the things you value most, because those are the things in life you will defend most passionately.

And make no mistake—it's intentional.

The easiest way for them to suck you in is to accuse you of doing things that they themselves did. It's almost too easy for you to point out the hypocrisy. And that's the point—yes, it's too easy. Because it's a trap. If you have a perfect retort to their garbage, there's a reason for that. Do not fall for it. They want you on the defensive, trying to prove yourself to everyone. Once you've taken the bait, their job is done.

Boredom

When you're having a bad day, sometimes you just need to be on your own to recharge and figure things out. Maybe you like to use your alone time to create, write, cook, imagine, meditate, paint, or dream. Or maybe you're just looking to take a well-deserved nap. My point is, whether you're an introvert or extrovert, occasional quiet time seems to be a universal human need.

But this is not the case with psychopaths.

Alone time may be one of the few things that truly agitates these people, who are otherwise seamlessly cool and calm. Without a conscience, there's not very much to think about on their own. And without people spoon-feeding them adoration and attention, the boredom sets in quickly.

Psychopaths are always bored, and they constantly seek out stimuli to distract themselves from this nagging condition. They cannot tolerate being alone for any extended period of time. Healthy human beings learn to enjoy quiet time and introspection—this is how we discover some of the most important things about ourselves. Psychopaths, on the other hand, have nothing to discover. They spend their free time mirroring others and copying desirable traits. Empathy allows us to experience imagination and creativity, two of the most wonderful human qualities that psychopaths can only mimic.

In various forums devoted to self-proclaimed sociopaths, there are frequent discussions about how to cope with the overwhelming boredom that consumes their daily life. Not surprisingly, most of the answers have to do with sex, alcohol, drugs, and—of course—manipulating others.

Relationships provide the psychopath with the most stable and reliable form of boredom relief, because once they have you hooked, they can reach out to you at any time for compliments, attention, and praise. And once they have other targets readily available, they're safe to start emotionally abusing you, which is far more interesting than pretending to love you. Watching you scurry around like a rat in a maze provides them with an entertaining distraction from their otherwise insufferably boring life. The idealization phase is merely a by-product of this boredom—a necessary step in grooming you so that they can abuse you for as long as possible.

At times in the relationship, you may have felt exhausted because it seemed like you never had any alone time with your partner after the honeymoon period. It was always spending time with them and their friends, from one busy plan to the next. Psychopaths also have a tendency to behave like innocent children, surrounding themselves with maternal and paternal types who constantly want to be there for them, offering support and providing for them at every turn.

These people are all kept around to alleviate the psychopath's boredom. The more targets the better. At first, the psychopath might have complained about them to you. But after you're locked into the relationship, the psychopath will oscillate between choosing you and choosing others in order to keep everyone on their toes. No matter who they choose for the day, one thing is certain: they will not spend time on their own. It's far better to provoke hurt feelings in you and watch your reactions than to simply sit alone in their room for an hour.

Eventually, the most hurtful boredom comes when it seems that they have suddenly lost all interest in you. Everything you do seems to bore them. As you struggle to regain their attention, you find that the qualities they once admired in you have apparently become glaring faults. Nothing you do seems to bring back the intense focus they once aimed at you—the time when you were the *only* one who could cure all of that boredom.

Even after they begin treating you terribly, a part of you may wish that you could win back your place as "Boredom Relief #1." This is completely normal, because once you realize that the idealization phase is gone forever, the next best option is to frantically ensure that you at least remain one of their many sources of entertainment.

Yes, this is how warped our standards become.

Covert Gossiping

The psychopath claims to hate "drama," but you will slowly come to find that there's more drama surrounding their life than anyone you've ever known. Of course, according to them, none of this is actually their fault. People just love them too much, treat them badly, and always seem to go crazy around them. How unfair for them.

But, as we're beginning to discover, that's not really the case.

The psychopath is constantly provoking drama, rivalries, and competitions. What separates them from everyday drama queens is their ability to appear innocent in all of it. They make subtle suggestions, then sit back and watch as others go down in flames for them. This is where the "covert" part comes into play.

They plant little seeds of poison, whispering to everyone, idealizing them to their face, and then insulting them behind their backs. "Insulting" doesn't really even capture the subtlety of a psychopath's gossip. Instead of overtly trashing people, psychopaths paint themselves as victims. Someone is always wronging them in one way or another. So instead of being a backstabbing gossiper, they come across as a sympathetic victim of everyone else's bad behavior. At some point, you might have even felt special being the one they chose to complain to (again, that's how screwed up our standards become).

But then you end up on the receiving end of it.

Suddenly *you're* the villain—the one causing them all this pain and torment. This process begins in earnest once the relationship starts to unravel. They begin running back to the very same people they once complained about to you, using them to lament about how crazy you've become. This generates a lot of sympathy, which is the perfect way to transition to their next target without anyone judging their blatant infidelity.

During the relationship, you probably found yourself disliking and resenting people you'd never even met. Could that have anything to do with the psychopath's constant suggestions that these people were all in love with them, wanted them, abused them, or were jealous of you? Over time, this builds up so much negativity and envy—more than you'd experience in any healthy relationship. And the sad part is, this same negativity is also felt toward *you* by everyone else.

The Manipulator Test

If you're looking for a way to discern manipulators from empathetic people, pay attention to the way they speak about others in relation to you. Kind, decent people will go out of their way to make sure you know their friends and family members really like you. Manipulators, on the other hand, will always seek to triangulate. They provoke rivalries and jealousy by manufacturing competitions. They whisper in your ear that their friend, an ex, or a family member is very jealous of you—or maybe that they said something nasty about you. Make no mistake, they're whispering the exact same things about you to those very same people. So ask yourself, does this person create harmony, or do they engineer chaos?

Sure, friends and exes might smile to your face, just like you smile to theirs. But deep down, everyone under the psychopath's spell is harboring this growing resentment toward one another. And it's not for any legitimate reason—it's because you've been turned against each other. You're all just movable pawns in the game the psychopath plays for attention and drama. They keep each target far enough apart that you can't compare notes, but close enough that you're always on edge and unsure of where you stand.

As impossible as it might seem while you're still involved with a psychopath, all of these people are probably perfectly nice human beings. Like you, they've just been poisoned and brainwashed to believe the worst about everyone else. Most empathetic partners are excited to befriend their partner's friends and make a positive impression. This was probably true at the beginning of the relationship, but as the triangulation and gossip worsened, you started to experience more and more negative emotions. And perhaps you blamed yourself, believing that you were becoming an unrecognizable mess of jealousy and resentment.

This is what happens when you enter the psychopath's reality—all of their gossip and lies start to distort your own reality. Because here are the two realities you must choose from:

1. The psychopath is normal. Everyone else is jealous, ill-intentioned, and self-serving.

2. The psychopath is jealous, ill-intentioned, and self-serving. Everyone else is normal.

During the idealization and love-bombing, we favor option one. It all feels absolutely incredible, and so we begin to define a new reality around our "soul mate." They are wonderful, everyone else is wonderful. Life is good! But then the covert gossip begins, and that's when our reality starts to shift. In order for us to continue living in the dream reality, where the psychopath is honest and good, all of their gossip must also be true. All of these other people must be jealous, ill-intentioned, and self-serving. Because if that's not true, then that means the psychopath is a liar, gossiper, and manipulator.

The stronger this reality becomes, the harder it is to break away from it. It really does start to feel like all of these people are against you—and that's how the psychopath wants you to feel. Because then your entire sense of happiness is dependent on them. And what's more, maintaining a false reality requires that you make a lot of excuses and explanations that keep you on the defensive and in denial. This is an extremely effective distraction (and de-stabilizer) from the frightening truth that your idealizer is actually your enemy.

During the breakup and recovery, we're ripped away from option one—which was really just a fantasy—and faced with reality. We feel devastated, empty, and hopeless. Without that fantasy, we've lost *everything*. We've lost the most important, wonderful, perfect partner in the entire world. And on top of that, everyone else is untrustworthy and toxic. We have nobody and nothing.

But then we start to put the pieces together and experience small moments of trust with the people around us. This is where a Constant can truly change someone's life. We see how we feel around someone who treats us well. We notice the freedom in spending time with someone who is not judging, triangulating, or spreading lies. Eventually, we start to place the negativity where it really belongs, instead of shifting it onto the rest of the world.

And finally, everything falls into place.

Reality number two strengthens. The first option doesn't even make sense anymore. It was never you and your partner against the world—it was only your partner against you. You begin to find peace and feel compassion toward people you once disliked. The cognitive dissonance lessens as you spend more time in the proper reality, away from the psychopath's web of lies. Your natural mercy and empathy return to you. Manufactured paranoia transforms into genuine trust, and at long last, the distractions are gone so that you can turn your focus to the *real* problem.

Torture by Triangulation

To draw you closer, the psychopath creates an aura of desirability— of being wanted and courted by many. It will become a point of pride for you to be the preferred object of their attention, to win them away from a crowd of admirers. They manufacture the illusion of popularity by surrounding themselves with members of the opposite sex: friends, former lovers, and your eventual replacement. Then they create triangles that engender rivalries and raise their perceived value. (Adapted from *The Art of Seduction* by Robert Greene.)

The psychopath gleefully create love triangles, surrounding themselves with other targets to manufacture competition and make themselves seem in high demand at all times. Some targets will be used just to make you jealous, while others will be groomed as your replacement. After once texting you on a minute-by-minute basis and declaring you their "perfect" soul mate, they begin to pull away, showering other targets with this very same attention. This causes you to try harder, striving to win them back—unaware that they are simply toying with you. Meanwhile, the new victim falls fast, believing you to be "crazy" and "bipolar" and "abusive." But despite this sickening smear campaign, the psychopath will still flatter you behind closed doors in order to give you a glimmer of hope—keeping you hooked until the bitter end.

A note before I continue: People fall in and out of love. People find new love, before and after relationships come to an end. People cheat on one another. This section is not about these everyday occurrences—no matter how heartbreaking and unfair they might be. Instead, I am describing a very specific set of patterns and behaviors that psychopaths utilize in order to torture and control their targets.

Psychopaths, like most predators, seek power and control. They want to dominate their partners sexually, emotionally, and physically. They do this by exploiting vulnerabilities. This is why they love-bomb you with attention and flattery in the beginning of the relationship—because no matter how strong or confident you are, being in "love" makes you vulnerable. Psychopaths don't need physical aggression to control you (although sometimes they resort to it). Instead, relationships provide them with the perfect opportunity to consume you by manufacturing the illusion of love. This is why it's so damaging when bystanders say, "Well, why didn't you just leave?" You never entered a relationship with the psychopath expecting to be abused, belittled, and criticized. You were tricked into falling in love, which is the strongest human bond in the world. Psychopaths know this.

So how do psychopaths maintain such a powerful hold over

their targets? One of their favorite methods is through triangulation. When I mention this term, survivors usually equate it with the next target, but that is not always the case. Psychopaths use triangulation on a regular basis to seem in high demand, and to keep you obsessed with them at all times. This can occur with anyone:

Your family
Their family
Your friends
Their friends
Ex-partners
Partners-to-be
Complete strangers

The psychopath's ability to groom others is unmatched. They feel an intense euphoria when they turn people against each other, especially when it's over a competition for them. The psychopath will manufacture situations to make you jealous and question their fidelity. In a normal relationship, people go out of their way to prove that they are trustworthy—but the psychopath does exactly the opposite. They are constantly suggesting that they might be pursuing other options, or spending time with other people, so that you can never settle down into a feeling of peace. And they will always deny this, calling you crazy for bringing it up.

The issue here is that you're accustomed to such a high level of attention after they first lured you in that it feels very personal and confusing when they direct that attention elsewhere. They know this. They'll "forget" plans with you, and spend a few days with friends whom they always complained about to you. They'll ignore you to spend more time with their family, when they initially told you that they were all horrible people. They'll seek sympathy from an ex when a member of their family dies, and explain that they just have a "special friendship" you wouldn't understand. Often—if not always—that ex is someone they previously claimed was abusive and unstable.

Seeking attention, sympathy, and solace from people who are not you is a very common tactic of the psychopath. As an empathetic person, and as their partner, you rightfully feel that they should be seeking comfort in you. You've always healed them in the past, so what's different now? They once claimed that they were a broken person, and that you were the reason they were happy again. But now they turn to private friendships or past relationships that you could "never understand." And they will always make sure to shove this in your face.

This brings me to the next topic: social media.

Technology makes it so much easier for the psychopath to manipulate through triangulation. It can be as simple as liking a comment from an old ex, while ignoring one from you. They will "accidentally" upload a photo album where they're embracing the ex they once claimed to hate. Everything appears to be unintentional—you often attribute it to insensitivity—but make no mistake: it is carefully calculated.

They will strategically post ambiguous statuses, songs, and videos that suggest you might be "losing" them. They will share things that are intentionally meant to lure in new and old targets—for example, an inside joke with their new victim, or the love song that they once shared with their ex. This does two things: It leaves you feeling unhinged, anxious, and jealous. But it also makes the competing party feel confident, loved, and special. They are grooming others as they erode your identity—two birds with one stone.

They want you to confront them about these things, because they are so seemingly minimal that you will appear crazy and jealous for bringing them up. They will calmly provide an excuse for everything and then blame you for creating drama. Covert abuse is impossible to prove, because it's always strategically ambiguous. You can't prove that they're luring in their ex because of a song they posted, but you know it intuitively. This is how they accomplish the crazy-making. Because let's be honest: complaining about Facebook statuses and comments does seem immature. That's exactly how they want you to feel.

Exes who maintain a "friendship" with the psychopath do not understand that they are puppets to the psychopath. Instead, they feel that they are fulfilling some sort of beautiful duty as a friend—someone who will always be there for them. They don't understand that they are only kept around to spice things up when the psychopath becomes bored. They don't see that they are the basis of so many fights—not because their friendship with the psychopath is special and desirable, but because the psychopath intentionally creates that drama. They are operating under the delusion that their friendship with the psychopath is brilliant, unique, and unprecedented. When in reality, they are just used for triangulation.

Psychopaths are also expertly skilled at surrounding themselves with givers—insecure people who find self-worth in taking care of others. This is why your giving seems so insignificant and replaceable during the relationship. They will seem to adore people who are nothing like you—sometimes even the exact opposite of you. The message is simple: You are no longer special. You are replaceable. If you don't give them the worshiping they deserve, they'll always have other sources. And even if you do give them positive energy, they'll get bored with you eventually. They don't need you. Their current round of fans will always spoil and admire them, making you believe that they truly must be a great person. But take a careful look around. You'll notice that all the fans seem to have an unspoken air of misery about them.

The final triangulation happens when they make the decision to abandon you. This is when they'll begin freely talking about how much this relationship is hurting them, and how they don't know if they can deal with your behavior anymore. They will usually mention talking to a close friend about your relationship, going into details about how they both agreed that your relationship wasn't healthy. In the meantime, they've been blatantly ignoring frantic messages from you. You'll be sitting there wondering why they aren't talking with you about these concerns, considering it's *your* relationship.

Well, the reason is that they've already made the decision to dump you—now they're just torturing you. They only seek advice from people they know will agree with them. That "friend" they're talking to is probably their next target.

There are three main characters in a psychopath's love triangle, and with each one, the psychopath must wear a specific mask and act a certain way:

1. **You:** Instead of feeling shameful like most normal people would, when the psychopath cheats they actually go out of

their way to ensure you know about their infidelities—without ever admitting to them, of course. This involves openly flirting with others (often over Facebook), bragging to you about all of the people who want to sleep with them, and calling you crazy and jealous when you react accordingly. With you, the psychopath acts covert, ambiguous, condescending, and always trying to keep you doubting the relationship.

2. **The New Target:** The psychopath is not interested in torturing the new target yet. Instead, they use your impending self-destruction to lure in the next victim, the "favorite." As you begin to fall apart, it is easy to point at your desperate texts and evoke sympathy from the new target because of how crazy you've gotten. The psychopath will put the new target on a pedestal, explaining how much happier they feel now. The new target will feel elated, being the one to save the psychopath from their supposedly abusive partner (you). The mask the psychopath dons is one that makes them appear innocent, victimized (by you), and in need of saving (from you). At the same time, they are extremely complimentary and grateful to the new target, whom they credit with restoring their happiness.

3. **The Fan Club:** The psychopath also needs to keep a close watch on their supply of friendships. Even the least perceptive person in the world could notice when a relationship coup is happening. So instead of openly cheating and replacing one victim for another, the psychopath must be more careful. They will engage in serious talks with their

friends about how much the current relationship is hurting them, and start to hand out shallow praise as a way to ensure loyalty. This is preliminary damage control, to make sure they remain in a favorable light even after the obvious cheating. They want to be sure their fan club is there to clap louder than ever when they put the new target on display, showing just how perfect their new life is. Every bit of support they get from their friends further confounds you. You wonder how in the world anyone could support this person. With their fan club, the psychopath is schmoozing, charming, looking for sympathy, and ultimately acting very cheerful when it comes time to parade the new target, receiving all of the support and congratulations they crave.

The Following

No matter how much they abuse their partners, toxic people will always have a loyal following of fans cheering for everything they do. These people are blinded by shallow flattery that the manipulators use to control them. Fan clubs change often, as psychopaths' friendships are neither deep nor meaningful in any way. All that matters is constant attention and adoration. Anyone who fails to provide this mindless reinforcement will promptly be replaced with someone who can.

Think about the amount of calculation and planning it must take to pull this off. Psychopaths are cunning, cold, and very aware of their own behavior. They take on three different personas in order to make you doubt your own sanity!

After the breakup, when most normal people would feel very embarrassed and secretive about entering a new relationship so quickly, the psychopath will openly brag about how happy they are with their new partner. And even more surprising, they fully expect you to be happy for them. Otherwise you are bitter and jealous.

During this period, they make a postdump assessment. If you grovel or beg, they are likely to find some value in your energy. They will be both disgusted and delighted by your behavior. If you lash out and begin uncovering their lies, they will do everything in their power to break you down. Even if you come back to them later with an apology, they will permanently despise you for daring to talk back to them. You've seen too much—the predator behind the mask.

Even after the relationship is over, they will use triangulation to try to drive you insane. They'll wave their new partner in your face, posting pictures and declaring their happiness online. They want to prove how happy and perfect they are together, but more than that, they want you to hate the new target so you blame him or her for the dissolution of your relationship, instead of the true abuser.

So how can you protect yourself from this devastating emotional abuse? First, you must learn self-respect. I will discuss this in more detail later on in the book. But the bottom line is, you need to know what is acceptable and unacceptable behavior in a relationship. You should know that a partner who cheats and antagonizes is not worth your time. You should never resort to calling yourself crazy in order to account for their extremely dicey behavior. But that's hard to do with subtle, covert, crazy-making abuse.

So here's where I introduce "The Detective Rule." The idea is simple: if you find yourself playing detective with someone, you should remove them from your life immediately. Remember your Constant? Do you play detective with them? Do you cyberstalk their Facebook page and question everything they say and do? No, of course not. So you know the inclination to do that with your partner is not about you—something is compelling you to feel wary and suspicious.

Even if this sense of distrust feels obscure and unreasonable, trust your gut. If you are constantly worrying or doubting your thoughts, it's time to stop second-guessing yourself and start taking action.

Miraculously, every single time you remove that toxic person from your life, you will find that the anxiety subsides. Only *you* can truly know if someone is harming you. Only *you* know what is best for you. You can decide whether or not you like the way you feel around someone. No one can ever tell you that your feelings are wrong. Remember the question: How are you feeling today? The answer is all that matters.

Triangulation leaves long-lasting emotional wounds, and it makes you feel as if you are a jealous, needy, insecure monster. Start healing those wounds and understand that your insecurities were manufactured. You were not yourself—you were manipulated. The real you is kind, loving, open-minded, and compassionate. You do not need to question these things anymore.

The Detective

When dealing with liars and manipulators, we often find ourselves playing "detective." This is your intuition telling you that something is deeply wrong with the individual you're investigating. For some reason, their actions never seem to match up with their words. You find them constantly making excuses and blaming others, even though their stories never actually add up. You become lost in confusing conversations that somehow result in you being labeled jealous, overly sensitive, and paranoid. But when all is said and done, you will look back on every single instance where they called you crazy and realize that they were lying to your face. Every excuse was covering up yet another con, infidelity, or even a completely pointless lie (the ones they tell for fun). Psychopaths are skilled at covert abuse, leading you on a scavenger hunt that makes you doubt everything about your once easygoing nature.

Silence

Silence is one of the most powerful tools of identity erosion. It is covert punishment, intended to manipulate a change in behavior without actually appearing to be overtly manipulative. When empathetic people are given the silent treatment, they often self-destruct and think of everything they might have done wrong. As a result, they start to whittle down their entire personalities in order to avoid repeating any of those potential wrongdoings.

The silent treatment is a brutal form of abuse—one that pits you against your own mind. You declare war on your intuition and everything that you know to be true. Once your identity has been sufficiently eroded, the psychopath can use this final technique without any chance that you'll leave them. Instead, you will torture yourself, carrying out the remainder of the abuse for them.

They will leave you alone with your thoughts, planting subtle hints and suggestions over social networking to encourage your paranoia. You will run through everything you've done in the relationship, blaming yourself for your feelings and emotions. You will wake up in the middle of the night, heart racing as you hope for a text from them. Nothing. You log onto Facebook and see them chatting away with friends and exes. They're not unavailable; they're ignoring you.

You will be expected to understand that they may not talk for days on end, despite having texted you on an hourly basis in the beginning of the relationship. You will begin to feel that you are on "probation," despite having no idea what you've done wrong. You may become passive-aggressive, drafting out long emails about their changed behavior and complete lack of contact. You might even feel strongly enough to suggest a break, but you will never follow through with it for more than a few hours. You will think you can out-ignore the psychopath, remaining calm and collected, as if nothing is wrong, so you don't appear clingy. But they will always win this game. Because they do not need your attention—they have already found someone else. Yes, when the psychopath begins ignoring you for days, it means they've found a new target. Otherwise, they would continue focusing all of their efforts on you. But now you are just an obstacle. They've found something new and exciting and your emotions are just a bothersome speed bump in their latest romantic venture. But they will never tell you this. They will just continue to read your desperate text messages, ignoring them without another word. They will lash out and accuse you of being obnoxious, crazy, and clingy. They will refuse to discuss anything over the phone or in person, unless it happens entirely on their terms. The abuse is no longer covert. Their contempt for you is unmistakable.

But despite all of this, they will not dump you. Not yet. They're saving that for the right moment.

The Grand Finale

The psychopath carefully selects the most indifferent and heart-breaking way imaginable to abandon you. They want you to self-destruct, as they begin the grooming process with their latest victim. They destroy you as a way to reassure themselves that their new target is better. But most importantly, they destroy you because they hate you. They despise your empathy and love—qualities they must pretend to feel every single day. To destroy you is to temporarily silence the nagging reminder of the emptiness that consumes their soul.

The Aftermath

Psychopaths latch on to successful people and steal what they have worked hard to attain. If you have a solid career, the psychopath will sponge from your income and avoid finding a job of their own. If you have a great group of friends, the psychopath will charm them into their fan club, ultimately turning them against you. They will end up sucking everything out of your life, and once they've taken everything you have to offer, they will find a new host.

The psychopath plans their discarding of you to be hurtful and confusing, causing you to feel completely worthless. And then you watch as their new life unfolds before your very eyes, leaving you to wonder what in the world just happened. Nothing from their patronizing breakup excuse makes sense. None of it adds up. Looking back, you will find that this person offered absolutely nothing of value to the relationship—only false praise and flattery, to keep you from catching on to their extremely parasitic lifestyle. Psychopaths leave behind nothing but pain, confusion, and chaos in their path of destruction.

The Psychopathic Breakup Checklist

The psychopath almost always has a new target lined up to replace their current partner. But instead of simply ending your relationship and entering the new one, they act out the items on the psychopathic breakup checklist:

1. Covertly sprinkle hints that they are interested in someone else.

2. Repeat Step 1 until you finally react.

3. Calmly imply that you are being oversensitive and jealous.

4. Give you the silent treatment for being sensitive and jealous.

5. Repeat Step 4 until you start to self-destruct.

6. Use your self-destruction to convince the new target that you're crazy, that way the new target doesn't feel like their cheating is "wrong."

7. Use your self-destruction to convince their friends that you're crazy; that way they have full support from their fan club when they replace you.

8. Begin to patronize you and explain how much your unstable behavior is hurting them.

9. Choose the most insensitive way imaginable to dump you.

10. Wave the new target in your face to show how happy they are without you.

Normal breakups never happen like this, but psychopaths want to ensure that they seem innocent while you appear to be the monster. Even though they are the ones who are cheating and lying, these steps turn the tables around so that they can play victim and make sure that you are left with absolutely nothing.

Setup

The discarding process will feel casual and impulsive, but make no mistake—it has been planned for weeks, if not months. During this process, you will begin to feel that they actually want *you* to dump *them*. They will go out of their way to upset and harm you, and you will know in your heart that they have no interest in continuing the relationship. But of course, they will never say this. They will deny any suggestions you might have about their intentions. Instead, they will unload all of the blame on you, making you feel that your self-destructive behavior is what's really ruining the relationship—not their blatant abuse tactics.

While you're frantically running around trying to fix things, they will be courting their next target. They may already be sleeping together. And they'll make sure you suspect it—dropping hints and innuendos until you can't take it anymore and just explode. Then they'll use your increasingly volatile behavior as a pity ploy for their next victim. What better way to convince them of your insanity than to present them with your seemingly unprovoked and hysterical text messages?

You will spend all of this time thinking that they've just lost interest, or that your jealousy issues extinguished the spark. Months into recovery, things will finally start to click. You will be able to look back at their prebreakup performance and put all of the pieces into place. You will be shocked—unable to comprehend such a cunning scheme. You will be disgusted when you realize how long you were strung along. You will wonder why they didn't just dump you the moment they met someone new. You will realize that they were blatantly ignoring you—not because they were busy with work—but because they were busy in bed.

And all the while, they made *you* feel like the monster.

Destruction

To a psychopath's target, the sudden breakup seems to come out of nowhere. But to the psychopath, this moment has been carefully planned for quite some time. They've been spreading lies and gossip about you, quietly convincing others that you're unstable and ruining the relationship. They use this story to groom the next victim and distract friends from their obvious cheating. You will find yourself replaced in a matter of days, watching as their "perfect" life unfolds with someone else. While you were running around desperately trying to repair things, they were already starting up another relationship. And instead of breaking up with you like a normal human being, they strung you along until the bitter end. They deemed you "crazy" and "jealous," gleefully eroding your entire identity as they pranced off with someone else. Psychopaths don't just break up with their targets—they use breaking up as an opportunity to watch you self-destruct: physically, emotionally, and spiritually.

The Talk

When the psychopath breaks up with you, it will feel nonchalant and disingenuous. They might even do it over a text message to make you feel completely worthless. They will talk mostly about themselves and their "feelings"—explaining that they just can't go on like this anymore. You will remain paralyzed and numb throughout the conversation. You knew it was coming, but you just can't believe it happened. You will hear a lot of word salad about their ex and your changed behavior, but nothing about the target they're replacing you with. They will appear both pitiful (of you) and oddly cheerful.

They will choose the most inconvenient setting possible in which to dump you. If you live cross-country, they will have no problem letting you come out to visit them, only to dump you halfway through the trip. By disrupting your travel plans and removing you from familiar surroundings, they ensure that you will be completely unhinged by the news—adding to the confusion and inferiority that you already feel.

You will leave the breakup feeling nothing but emptiness. I cannot describe this feeling as depression, because it is worse than that. In this moment, you will feel that your spirit has died.

Abandonment

Sudden abandonment is not normal behavior. If someone truly feels all of the love and passion they proclaim, they will not be able to disappear months later without another word. The person who once declared you better than all of their crazy exes now grooms a new target by painting *you* as the crazy ex. Everything that comes out of a psychopath's mouth is manufactured garbage. This becomes especially apparent when they migrate from the personality mirroring—"we're just the same in every way"—to the inevitable abandonment, when they begin to mirror an entirely different person. Once you start to understand how this cycle works, you will realize that you have not lost your soul mate at all. While they continue this cycle forever, you begin a new adventure, free from the never-ending lies and mind games of the soulless.

Triangulation Again

The psychopath isn't done with you yet. Their favorite time to triangulate is right after the breakup. After they change their relationship status to "Single" on Facebook, you'll think that things can't possibly get any worse. You have friends asking how you're doing, but you're not able to focus on anything except your ex-partner. Looking at their pictures makes you feel sick, but you keep doing it anyway. You scroll through old memories, impulsively deleting what you can—immediately regretting it.

And then you see it.

A few days after the breakup, they're posting pictures of themselves with someone else. Someone you've never seen before. They make no effort to hide their latest conquest. In fact, it feels like they're showing the new target off. They feel no embarrassment and no guilt. You know it's a bad idea, but your curiosity gets the best of you: you start peeking around, discovering that this new person has been interacting with your ex for a while now. They've been joking around and subtly flirting on social media, but you never noticed. You were probably completely focused on the ex before you.

Before you know it, they've changed their relationship status and their friends are all enthusiastically congratulating the happy couple. They've clearly known about the new partner for some time. While you were written off as the crazy ex, the next target was already preparing to take your place. The psychopath's fan club cheers for them, clapping louder than ever before—their hero has found the (latest) love of his or her life.

Superiority Complex

After the breakup and triangulation, the psychopath feels an immense amount of superiority. This is when they're at their "best"—glowing with energy as they watch you fall from grace. They put their newest target on display because they want you to know about her or him. They're waiting for your reaction, and if you don't react, they will invent a reason to talk to you, making sure their latest profile picture is displayed front and center. Oftentimes, the psychopath will use pointless requests as an excuse to get your attention. For example, they may say they want to return an article of clothing or a DVD—something that any normal person would just forget about.

Once they have your attention, they will adopt a calm, patronizing demeanor, talking down to you as if they're some kind of relationship guru because they're happy and you're single. During the whole conversation, they will take on a very arrogant, "I'm in charge" sort of attitude. After the breakup, they're obsessed with being the calm and superior person. The winner.

They will minimize everything that happened, warning you not to create any drama. Instead of apologizing for their abusive behavior and now-obvious cheating, they make sweeping statements explaining that breakups are just difficult. They depersonalize the experience and speak down to you as if they pity you. They use this pseudo pleasantry to come across as the bigger person. They will wish you all the best, playing it off casually, making it seem as if this was just an everyday breakup.

If you don't allow them the postbreakup superiority routine, they will become extremely unpleasant. They do not want to talk about their infidelity or lies. They want you to idolize them in your memory. And remember how they gave you the silent treatment for entire days at the end of your relationship? Well, they still expect prompt responses from you—otherwise you're labeled bitter and jealous.

If you feel like punching a wall by this point, you're in good company.

The Emotional Abuser's Trap

Psychopaths, narcissists, and sociopaths are experts at flattery and charm. Although it feels amazing at first, this idealization is actually responsible for most of the damage when the relationship comes crashing down. They set a trap, and it's a trap that no un-suspecting victim could hope to escape from.

1. **By idealizing you, the psychopath can expect this attention and adoration to rebound very quickly.** Their love-bombing ultimately results in a very quick bond, one where you fall fast and give back all of the "love" you are receiving. In your mind, this individual truly becomes the most passionate, perfect soul mate you could ever imagine. You feel and express this love on a daily basis.

2. **You share your excitement about this relationship with all of your friends and family.** Oftentimes, they already have a front-row seat for this constant flattery. Sites like Facebook ensure that the mutual idealization is visible to the world. It feels good to have our egos stroked, ignited by all of this public praise.

3. **The emotional abuser slowly begins to back away.** At first it's subtle. You can't quite put your finger on it, but something feels different. They don't text or call quite as often, they seem less interested, you start to feel like a chore, and they're always late to see you. However, due to what is described in paragraphs one and two above, you are determined to continue the idealization. You ignore the worsening behavior and actually idealize them further, hoping to restore your dream. You don't want to be like their crazy ex; you want to be easygoing and forgiving.

4. **You continue to tell your friends, family, and self just how amazing your partner is.** Even though the relationship is getting progressively worse, you're sure that enough love and positive energy will fix everything. At this point, the psychopath can do whatever they desire, and you will continue to speak highly of them.

5. **The psychopath's abuse becomes much worse.** The triangulation begins. You are punished through silence and criticism. You are called crazy and hypersensitive. And eventually, you are abandoned. Throughout all of this, you continue your desperate attempts to save the relationship. You find yourself crying, pleading, and denying reality. This person has become your entire life. You have no one to reach out to for help, because they all believe your relationship to be perfect.

6. **After the abandonment, you begin to put the puzzle pieces together.** You discover psychopathy through a Google search and start thinking, "Oh my God, this is uncanny." The more you learn, the angrier you get. Everything falls into place, you are validated beyond belief, and your truth has changed forever.

7. **The trap.** No one believes you. After all of your enthusiasm about the relationship, it doesn't make sense. How could you have been the victim of abuse? You were happy—you were elated. Your partner was amazing and treated you so well. You said it yourself! If things were really so bad, why

were you always praising them? Instead of being a victim, you sound crazy, bitter, and unable to handle rejection.

This is the emotional abuser's trap. They groom you to shower them with praise and adoration, so you effectively checkmate yourself once the abuse begins. Survivors often find their own friends taking the side of their abuser. It's devastating, and this trap is the final nail in the psychopathic coffin.

To avoid this, do not try to defend or explain yourself to anyone. Yes, you need to share your story, but you need to share it with people who know what you've been through. Stick to recovery forums and journals. If you seek out therapy, be sure the therapist understands the mind games of manipulators. He or she must be familiar with Cluster B personality disorders (which includes borderline personality disorder, narcissistic personality disorder, histrionic personality disorder, and antisocial personality disorder); otherwise you may just experience more victim blaming. You don't need someone telling you to "get over it" or "breakups are part of life." You need someone who will help you get out of this hell and set you on a path to peace.

You are not crazy. You're not bipolar, insane, hypersensitive, jealous, or needy. You're a survivor of emotional abuse—and you *can* escape this trap. Just remain calm, patient, and always kind to yourself. Someday you will be able to talk about this experience eloquently and believably. Do not worry about convincing others of your story right now. This is what the psychopath hopes for. By putting you on the defensive when you are at your most damaged, you end up looking guilty and unstable.

So say farewell to these games. You are not alone. Share your story with people who get it, and slowly you will find that this nightmare becomes nothing more than a strange, distant memory. The psychopath does not matter. It's the subsequent recovery journey that changes everything.

Why Are They So Happy with Someone Else?

This is probably one of the most common questions survivors ask during the early stages of recovery. After the breakup, the psychopath moves on very quickly to the target they already had lined up to replace you. On top of the cheating and lying, you're forced to take a front-row seat while they begin their "perfect" life with someone else.

If you believe they're treating the new target better than they treated you, you're not alone. This is how nearly every survivor feels (including the new target, when he or she inevitably gets replaced down the road). The psychopath presents an image of their new relationship that seems flawless, like a fairy tale. Before you know it, they've adopted someone else's dreams, likes, and dislikes. They're both flaunting the new relationship before the entire world, not even a hint of shame or guilt for the fact that you were essentially swapped out in a matter of days.

The emotional abuser appears to run happily off into the sunset with their next target, making you wonder if perhaps they really are capable of love. But there is never a happy ending with a psychopath. They'll gleefully parade their latest victim to the world in order to evoke jealousy and drama, which is already a sign that they haven't magically grown a conscience.

As you watch the new relationship unfold, you'll start to notice every little detail about the idealization—things you always wished for but never received. Perhaps they moved in with the new partner, even though they never wanted to live with you. Maybe they got married really quickly, after months of never quite being able to commit to you. They're probably posting endless pictures on Facebook, whereas you became more of a private aspect of their life. Basically, it feels like you were a bothersome speed bump along the way to their true fantasy.

But here's the difficult thing to understand: someone else was feeling the exact same way at the beginning of *your* relationship.

Every idealization is going to be different, which is why it always seems like the next person is getting something you didn't. Additionally, you're at rock bottom while the new target is on cloud nine, which makes the situation seem even more unfair.

The fact that the other person receives "special" treatment isn't an indication that there's anything wrong with you. And it's not the result of your reactions during the abuse or your supposed craziness. Even if you had behaved perfectly, the psychopath would have found some reason to abandon and replace you. All this idealization they're doing to someone else serves two simple purposes: (1) to groom the new target into a reliable source of attention and affection, and (2) to make you feel jealous and worthless by showering someone else with more love than they gave to you.

This is why it is so important to have no contact with your ex. If you continue to watch the new relationship unfold, you'll only torture yourself with more impossible questions and self-doubts. Every time you look, you'll end up wishing you hadn't. You'll wonder why this new relationship is lasting longer than yours did—why they're able to tolerate someone else for so much longer than they were with you. Because of all the triangulation during the abuse, you find yourself constantly comparing yourself with others, feeling inferior and inadequate because they've chosen someone else.

Don't waste your life waiting for something bad to happen in their new relationship. Because in the end, it won't make any difference. After the initial satisfaction, you'll still be left feeling all of these same awful emotions because your sense of self-worth is still entirely invested in someone else.

There is nothing wrong with you, and there's nothing inherently better about the new target. You're two entirely different people who were love-bombed and flattered, but it had absolutely nothing to do with your actual qualities or inner beauty. The idealization was a tool to gain control over you, and that is neither flattering nor validating—not for you, and not for anyone else. You might start to wonder who's more attractive, more successful, more intelligent, but none of that matters. When a psychopath sets their sights on a new target, that is where all of their energy will be focused. Even if you're the sexiest, funniest, smartest person in the world, you will be forgotten and ignored. It's not that you've actually lost any of these qualities, or that someone else has more good qualities than you. It simply means that you've run your course in terms of supplying positive attention. You were starting to question their lies, stand up for yourself, and dig into the truth. And because of that, you were punished.

It's okay to wonder why you weren't good enough or what you could have done differently. It's only human, considering what you're responding to. But the point of this book is to help you understand that you *are* good enough—that there was nothing you could have done differently. When it comes to psychopathic relationships, the abusive partner's behavior and choices have nothing to do with your best qualities. If anything, they train you to repress these qualities.

Now that you're free, you finally have the opportunity to explore these qualities for yourself and begin to cultivate a healthy self-respect. But you can only do this when you're not constantly comparing yourself to someone else. Most survivors find that they feel physically sick when they check in on their ex's new relationship—their heart goes into their throat and they can't even breathe right. Why would you subject yourself to this? Listen to your body, because it's trying to protect you. It knows that nothing good can come from keeping tabs.

If you can, make a No Contact calendar and encourage yourself to see how long you can make it without checking up on the new relationship. At PsychopathFree.com, every member starts with a "No Contact Counter" that tracks how long you've maintained no contact. You will find that the longer you go, the easier it gets. And before long, you might even start to develop a certain level of sympathy for the new target as you come to understand that this new relationship actually saved you from further abuse.

Happily Never After

The psychopath's new relationship may look perfect. You'll bear witness to the idealization of the new victim (they'll make sure you notice), and you will wonder what he or she offers them that you couldn't. But that "perfect pair" won't last long. Soon after the idealization, the psychopath will get bored. They always get bored. It is a constant, nagging affliction that consumes them. To temporarily alleviate it, they will begin to erode the new victim's identity—toying with him or her for some quick relief. Eventually, this isn't enough. They need more. They need to see their victim beg and plead. They need their victim to self-destruct. And thus the cycle of abuse repeats itself again and again. There is no need to wonder if they've somehow found true happiness without you. Anyone who treated you with such venom and contempt is not capable of suddenly loving another human being. These qualities are mutually exclusive.

In most cases, psychopaths are obsessed with making sure that they break up with their victims. This is a sign of power and control. But there are occasions when a survivor finally breaks free on their own, leaving the psychopath and liberating themselves from the abuse.

When the psychopath is the one who's discarded, you should prepare yourself for months—if not years—of stalking and harassment. Until they find another victim, they will pour all of their rage into ruining your life through intimidation and scare tactics. They will invent online personas to cyberstalk your Internet activity. This gives them the illusion of control—reassurance that you cannot exist without them.

They may also try to win you back. Don't be fooled. This is their final manipulative attempt to turn the tables—so that the dumping can occur on their terms. It sounds ridiculous that someone would go through the trouble of courting you just to dump you, but this is how psychopaths work.

Survivors often wish that their ex would make some form of contact, just for proof that they haven't been forgotten. But if your ex has moved on, consider yourself lucky. If you need any further confirmation of this, speak to someone who dumped a psychopath. You will hear their stories and quickly understand that your ex's silence is a wonderful gift.

The Irony

Strangely enough, the grand finale is also the psychopath's greatest tribute to your strength. It reveals their accidental respect for you. It seems impossible, because you're at rock bottom. You've never felt so worthless in your life. And this is exactly how the psychopath wants you to feel. So how can this be anything good?

There are four general cases that result in a grand finale. And in every single one of them, the psychopath is giving you an indirect compliment:

1. They've Found Another Partner

If the psychopath sees their new target as more valuable than you, what exactly does that say? It means that this new victim is more likely to provide them with the unconditional adoration that they crave. It also means you're not doing enough of that. When the psychopath dumps you for another target, they are writing you off as a less useful victim. They see you as less submissive, less controllable, and less vulnerable than their new target. When they dump you and rub the other partner in your face, they're not proving how happy they are; they're trying to erode your self-esteem so that they can convince themselves that you're worse than their new conquest.

The only time people need to prove their happiness to others is when they are, in fact, unhappy. When psychopaths triangulate you and post new pictures for the world to see, they're not happy. They're miserably and pathetically trying to convince themselves of a lie by manufacturing your downfall. They're complimenting you in their obsession with your failure.

2. You Caught Up with Their Lies

Did you ever hear this phrase: "God, you overanalyze everything"? Strange how your supposed overanalyzing was always a result of their cheating, lying, and triangulating. That phrase is the psychopath's way of making you feel crazy for pointing out the truth. When they punish you for pointing out their lies, they are once again complimenting you. By trying to destroy your sanity and intuition, they are telling you that these qualities of yours are currently too strong. They recognize these traits and try to convince you that they are weaknesses—ensuring that you won't rely on them anymore. If a psychopath accuses you of overanalyzing everything, it just means you're a good detective.

3. You're Too Happy

Psychopaths love to build people up in the idealization phase, but then they resent the happiness and love generated by their partners. Weird, right? It makes absolutely no sense. So the psychopath's solution is to harbor this resentment through passive-aggressive abuse. They make you feel unhinged and anxious, shattering all of the confidence that *they* built up. When they do this, they are flattering you. This means you embodied everything they hate: love, happiness, and joy. They despise these qualities because they're a reminder of everything they can never feel. Qualities they see as stupid and useless. Your smiles and laughter are a strange, nagging reminder that maybe being human is better than being soulless. To convince themselves otherwise, they plan the grand finale in order to make a mockery of these characteristics.

4. They're Bored with Your Emotions

Psychopaths love the idealization phase because everything is perfect. There are no problems, and they don't have to deal with anyone's dreaded emotions. But after they've tricked someone into falling in love with them, they suddenly find themselves in a strange predicament. Their victim loves them and wants to foster a greater emotional connection. The psychopath gets bored and uncomfortable with this very quickly. In these cases, the grand finale will often be about the victim being crazy, bipolar, or hysterical. Again, these are all a flattering way of saying: "Hey, you have a heart." But the psychopath hates things they do not understand, so they seek to destroy you. While you were spending so much time trying to repress your emotions in order to be the perfect partner, you were actually doing just fine as a regular person. Emotions are what make you human, and the psychopath got very tired of those human qualities.

Everything the psychopath values is the opposite of what you would value. So when they punish you, they're actually giving quite a tribute to the things you probably care about most. It's twisted and manipulative, because they convince you to doubt your greatest qualities—but looking back, you can begin to understand how this abuse was a subtle acknowledgment of your own strengths.

Granted, you probably don't want to hear any of that right

now. After the grand finale, there is no hope. No humor. No future. You have been deeply wounded by the pain this person inflicted upon you, and it will take years to fully comprehend the extent of the abuse. So turn the page, and we will walk this road together.

the path to recovery

Healing from psychopathic abuse is a long journey. It is neither linear nor logical. You can expect to swing back and forth between stages, perhaps even inventing a few of your own along the way. It is unlike the traditional stages of grief, because you have not truly lost anything—instead, you have gained everything. You just don't know it yet.

Why Does It Take So Long?

Breakups with abusers are much different from breakups with healthy human beings. Relationships with psychopaths take an unusually long time to recover from. Survivors often find themselves frustrated because they haven't healed as fast as they'd like. They also end up dealing with friends and professionals who give them well-intentioned advice about how it's "time to move on."

Whether you were in a long-term marriage or a quick summer fling, the recovery process will be the same when it comes to a psychopathic encounter. It takes twelve to twenty-four months to get your heart back in a good place, and even then, you might have tough days.

Please don't set a deadline for yourself. With time, you will begin to find moments of happiness, contentment, and hope. These moments will become stronger and more frequent through No Contact, as the abuser slowly drifts into a strange obscurity. In retrospect, this person likely won't even seem "real." You will

be unable to believe that you were ever caught up in such a frenzied panic, hooked by someone who mirrored your personality
and then triangulated you against others. Your heart and mind
have better things to focus on—namely, your own self-respect and
happiness.

No matter how long it takes, do not worry that you have been
permanently injured by this person. The empathetic spirit never
dies. It is always with you, and it will return in a new and beautiful form when it is ready. There will be ups and there will be
downs, but you are on a path to freedom that will last a lifetime.

The important thing here is to stop blaming yourself. Stop
wishing it would go faster. Stop thinking that the psychopath
somehow "wins" if you're still hurting. They are out of the picture
now. This journey is about you. If you come to peace with the
extended time line, you'll find this experience a lot more pleasant.
You can settle in, make some friends, and get cozy with this whole
recovery thing.

So why is it taking so long?

You Were in Love

Yes, it was manufactured love. Yes, your personality was mirrored
and your dreams manipulated. But you were in love. Love is the
strongest human emotion and bond in the world, and you felt it
with all your heart. It is always painful to lose someone you
loved—someone you planned to be with for the rest of your life.

The human spirit must heal from these love losses. Regardless
of your abuser's intentions, your love was still very real. It will

take a great deal of time and hope to pull yourself out of the standard postbreakup depression.

You Were in Desperate Love

Here's where we branch off from regular breakups. Psychopaths manufacture desperation and desire. You probably worked harder for this relationship than any other, right? You put more time, energy, and thought into it than ever before. And in turn, you were rewarded with the nastiest, most painful experience of your life.

In the idealization phase, they showered you with attention, gifts, letters, and compliments. They actually pretended to be exactly like you in every way. Everything you did was perfect to them. This made you elated, unaware that they were preparing you for the identity erosion.

You began to pick up on all sorts of hints that you might be replaced at any time. This encouraged your racing thoughts, ensuring that this person was on your mind every second of the day. This unhinged, unpredictable lifestyle is what the psychopath hopes to create with their lies, gaslighting, and triangulation.

By keeping them on your mind at all times, you fell into a state of desperate love. This is unhealthy, and not a sign that the person you feel so strongly about is actually worthy of your love. Your mind convinces you that if you feel so powerfully, then they must be the only person who will ever make you feel that way. And when you lose that person, your world completely falls apart. You enter a state of panic and devastation.

The Chemical Reaction

Psychopaths have intense emotional and sexual bonds with their victims. These are due to their sexual magnetism, and the way they train their victims' minds to become reliant upon their approval.

After they first adored you in every way, you let down your guard and began to place your self-worth in them. Your happiness started to depend on their opinion of you. Happiness is a chemical reaction going off in your brain—dopamine and receptors firing off to make you feel good.

Like a drug, the psychopath offers you this feeling in full force at the beginning. But once you become reliant on it, they begin to pull back. Slowly, you need more and more to feel that same high. You do everything you can to hang on to it, while they're doing everything in their power to keep you starving for their love and approval.

Inferiority and Comparison

There are thousands of support groups for survivors of infidelity. Infidelity leaves long-lasting insecurities and feelings of never being good enough. It leaves you constantly comparing yourself to others. That pain alone takes many people years to recover from.

Now compare this to the psychopath's triangulation. Not only do they cheat on you—they happily wave it in your face. They brag about it, trying to prove how happy they are with your replacement. They carry none of the usual shame and guilt that come with cheating. They are thrilled to be posting pictures and telling their friends how happy they are.

I cannot even begin to explain how emotionally damaging this is to someone who had once been the target of a psychopath's idealization. The triangulation alone will take so much time to heal from.

You Have Encountered Pure Evil

Everything you once understood about people did not apply to this person. During the relationship, you tried to be compassionate, easygoing, and forgiving. You never could have known that the person you loved was actively using these things against you. It just doesn't make any sense. And so you spent your time projecting a normal human conscience onto them, trying to explain away their inexplicable behavior.

But once you discover psychopathy, sociopathy, or narcissism, everything starts to change. You begin to feel disgusted—horrified that you let this darkness into your life. Everything clicks and falls into place. All of the "accidental" or "insensitive" behavior finally makes sense.

You try to explain this to friends and family members, but no one really seems to get it. This is why validation matters. When you come together with others who have experienced the same thing as you, you discover you are not crazy. You are not alone in this inhuman experience.

It takes a great deal of time to come to terms with this personality disorder. You end up having to let go of your past understanding of human nature, building it back up from scratch. You realize that people are not always inherently good. You begin to feel paranoid, hypervigilant, and anxious. The healing process is about learning to balance this new state of awareness with your once-trusting spirit.

Your Spirit Is Deeply Wounded

After the inevitable abandonment, most survivors end up feeling a kind of emptiness that cannot even be described as depression. It's like your spirit has completely gone away. You feel numb to everything and everyone around you. The things that once made you happy now leave you cold. You worry that your encounter with this monster has destroyed your ability to empathize, feel, and care.

I believe this is what takes the longest time to recover from. It feels hopeless at first, but your spirit is always with you. Wounded, for sure, but never gone. As you begin to discover self-respect and boundaries, it slowly starts to find its voice again. It feels safe opening up, peeking out sporadically to say hello. You will find yourself grateful to be crying again, happy that your emotions seem to be returning. This is great, and it will start to become more and more consistent.

Ultimately, you will leave this experience with an unexpected wisdom about the people around you. Your spirit will return stronger than ever before, refusing to be treated that way again.

You may encounter toxic people throughout your life, but you won't let them stay for very long. You don't have time for mind games and manipulation. You seek out kind, honest, and compassionate individuals. You know you deserve nothing less.

This newfound strength is the greatest gift of the psychopathic experience. And it is worth every second of the recovery process, because it will serve you for the rest of your life.

The Stages of Grief—Part I

The early stages of recovery are like a whirlwind—chaotic, volatile, and uncontrollable. During these stages, you likely don't even know that you encountered a psychopath. You blame yourself and feel that you will never be happy again. You act out in ways you never even imagined. You don't yet understand how the abuse destroyed your confidence and identity—because you don't even know to call it abuse. All you know is that you're hurting more than you ever have in your life. But no matter how fast this whirlwind spirals, you must not lose hope. You are not alone in this darkness, and everything is going to be okay.

Devastation

Symptoms: emptiness, shock, substance abuse, suicidal thoughts, inability to focus, depression, physical deterioration.

This is the stage immediately following the breakup, in which you feel all-consuming devastation. Your heart and mind become numb, and you are unable to perform trivial tasks. You've been ripped away from the chemical addiction going on in your brain, so you should expect to experience a lingering haze as you go through the withdrawal process. Your body will deteriorate and you will seem fragile and haunted when you look at yourself in the mirror. Before and after pictures of psychopathic abuse survivors are shocking.

Your sex drive will oscillate between desire for your ex and the misery of thinking about what you no longer have. Psychologically, you are extremely raw and vulnerable from the identity erosion, but at this point you aren't even aware that your identity was eroded. You don't yet understand the extent of the emotional abuse you have suffered. So instead of healing from their tactics, you are still a victim of them. You genuinely believe you deserve this—that you are nothing without them. That you are jealous, crazy, needy, clingy, and everything is your fault.

You feel worthless.

Emotionally, you will lose any connection you once had with the world around you. Your empathetic and perceptual abilities will temporarily collapse. Looking back, you will be unable to remember most of the details during this phase. Almost like an out-of-body experience, your mind will have blocked out many of the unbearably painful and embarrassing memories. A part of you shuts down in order to protect your spirit. The stages of grief are about bringing it to life again.

Taking Care of Yourself

During the entire healing process—but especially right now—you must remember to treat your body well. It's the least you can do, considering your mind is going to be out of commission for quite some time. Along the way, I'll make some more suggestions, but here are a few basic ideas to get you started:

1. Practice meditation whenever you can. My beautiful friend and ice-skating partner, An Old-Fashioned Girl, has shared many techniques on our website that you can try throughout the day. She offered one example where you simply take ten deep breaths in a row—and you can do this anytime, anywhere!

2. Take a multivitamin with B complex each day. This will ensure you're receiving all of the nutrients you need. B_6 and B_{12} can also help to combat depression.

3. Fish oil is an excellent supplement to keep your skin and hair strong, but it also has some great antidepressant qualities.

4. Exercise! Go for a walk each day. Spend half an hour at the gym. Don't worry if your workout is less intense than it used to be. To this day, my friends still refuse to go to the gym with me because I mostly just roll around on the exercise balls and giggle.

5. Eat three meals each day, even when you're not hungry. You probably won't feel like eating for a few weeks, but you

cannot starve your body. Keep yourself well fed and healthy.

6. Wake up at a reasonable hour each morning. You don't want to get stuck in the habit of rolling out of bed in the afternoon, too depressed to face the day. Set an alarm if you need to.

7. Get seven to nine hours of sleep. Adequate rest is essential to your mental health, and you won't be able to get through this if you're exhausted every day.

8. Go outside and get some sun. Wear sunscreen, of course, but enjoy the natural light of the outdoors, and absorb some vitamin D from the sun. You'll feel better.

9. Take care of your basic hygiene each day. Don't skip out on brushing your teeth or taking a shower. The more you get into a routine, the easier it will become to form good habits.

10. Get away from the mirror. Seriously, you look fine. The psychopath conditioned you to feel especially self-conscious about the way you look, but no one is judging you like they did.

Reflection

During the devastation period, you will find it very difficult to reflect on anything at all. But I must ask you to look inward, just for a moment.

This is the most important paragraph in the whole book. Please pay attention: Many survivors struggle with suicidal thoughts, unable to imagine life beyond this experience. To cope with this, some begin to drink alone or abuse prescription pills. If you're self-medicating or considering suicide, please put this book down and seek professional counseling immediately. No healing book or website can provide you with the help you need right now.

Even if you're not feeling suicidal, having professional guidance through this experience can be hugely beneficial. There are so many amazing psychologists, therapists, and counselors out there who transform lives every single day. Most of these people enter the field because they have an innate desire to help others. They'll usually list their specialties on their website. Try seeking out someone who specializes in the field of relationship abuse—off the bat, they'll understand that this is not a process to be rushed.

Everyone's going to have a different rapport with a therapist, but at the very least, this person should be compassionate, kind, and open-minded. You should never feel judged or uncomfortable speaking your mind. If you found any books or online articles that really resonated with your experience, you should feel welcome to bring them in for discussion.

After a few months with my therapist, I went from feeling suicidal and unable to get out of bed in the morning to being functional and eating again. I still had a long, long way to go, but she was the one who got me back on my feet when I had lost all hope. Sometimes we just need a little extra boost to get us out from that all-consuming darkness. There is absolutely no shame in reaching out a hand and asking for that help. You might be surprised to find that there are a lot of strangers willing to pull you back up.

Denial

Symptoms: volatility, pseudo happiness, manic moods, substance abuse, impulsivity, attention seeking, cyberstalking.

You can expect this stage to start up in full force when the psychopath begins waving their happy life in your face. You see them running off with another partner, gleefully telling the world how perfect their life is now. This triangulation is commonly done through social media. At this point, you aren't even angry about the new target because you likely have no idea how long the infidelity was going on. You just feel the need to prove that you are fine and dandy like the psychopath—because then maybe they'll want you back.

Realize that at this point, your healing is still largely centered around the psychopath desiring you again.

In order to convince yourself that everything is okay, you change jobs, spend money, and redefine your entire life. You lash out at everyone and everything except the psychopath. You go out drinking, partying, and dating recklessly—all in a monumental effort to convey the message that you are fine. You will become very impulsive, blowing away your savings and harboring delusional thoughts of returning to your idealizer. You may try to replicate the exact dynamic you had with the psychopath with another partner, only to get very frustrated that your sex life isn't as good or that they don't love-bomb you with attention.

You spend a lot of time online, peeking at their Facebook profile and learning about their new life. A part of you isn't ready or willing to believe that the relationship is actually over. You think if they just see one picture or comment of yours, then maybe they'll realize what a mistake they've made. But much to your dismay, they don't seem to be paying any attention to you at all. You might even invent fantasies in which they secretly want you back. So you continue to act out, unaware that your sense of self has become entirely consumed by someone else. This is the phase in which you'll be most likely to do things you'll regret after recovery has ended.

Drinking

Please stop drinking. In the early months of recovery, this might seem like the easiest way to deal with your pain. Downing a bottle of wine each night somehow becomes "normal"—and you defend it with excuses or a casual joke. But it's not funny. You are doing a lot of damage to your mind and body. If you're serious about healing, you need to be completely in touch with your sober, unaltered self. You will find no peace by indulging in alcohol-induced rants, drunk storytelling, and mindless partying. These distractions only serve to delay your healing process. You will still have all of the same work to do once you wake up the next morning—and it'll be made substantially more difficult by a hangover and embarrassing memories from the night before.

There's nothing wrong with having a drink every now and

then, but this experience is an exception. Spend a few months completely dry. Make a calendar if you need to, checking off each day as you go. You will be absolutely amazed at how quickly your healing process accelerates. Your mind is the most valuable tool in the recovery process—so treasure it and treat yourself kindly.

"If Only" Moments

A big part of the denial phase is still believing they must be interested because of how amazing things were when you were in love. It doesn't seem possible that they could already be in love with someone else (and it wouldn't be possible, in a normal relationship). You believe that what you had with them was unique and special, something that they frequently reminded you of during the relationship.

So instead of recognizing that things are over, you spend a lot of time wondering what you could have done differently to save your perfect relationship. You look back on every single moment that led to the "downfall" and wish that it hadn't gone that way. You think of creative ways to fix the things that you supposedly broke.

Here are some examples:

- "If only I hadn't confronted them about their ex, then we'd still be together."
- "If only I hadn't traveled that weekend, then they wouldn't have cheated on me."
- "If only I'd bought them a nice gift, then they would have realized how much I cared."

- "If only I hadn't asked them to stop criticizing me, then they wouldn't think I was so sensitive."
- "If only I'd pretended nothing was wrong when they gave me the silent treatment, then they wouldn't think I was so needy."
- "If only I wore a different outfit that day, then they would have found me more attractive."

What in the world! How would any of those things ever justify silence, cheating, abuse, or even dumping someone? And why should changing any of those minor events have any impact on whether or not a relationship succeeds? Love should be like a deep-rooted tree, not a sailboat. It should be stable and consistent, not conditional, based on changing situations—especially when half of your "mistakes" were perfectly reasonable reactions to unacceptable behavior.

If your entire relationship was hanging on a few "if only" moment going differently, then it was a terrible relationship. This means you were walking on eggshells, on the brink of a breakup any time something didn't go exactly according to plan. This is not companionship and support. It's like walking a tightrope with someone judging you the whole time, arms crossed, instead of extending a hand to help you safely to the other side. And if you fall down, then so be it. "If only" you hadn't.

But I'm getting ahead of myself. This is supposed to be the stages of grief, not Jackson arguing with his twenty-one-year-old self.

Just understand that these thoughts are completely normal, and they will start to subside as you dig deeper into psychopathy in the later stages of grief. If possible, please don't act on the "if only" moments. You might have an optimistic high where you suddenly dismiss this whole abuse thing, and think that one nice gesture or apology could fix everything. It won't. If this person really ever cared about you, you wouldn't be running every single one of your mistakes through your mind, wondering with each one if that was the reason you were replaced. This is what silence and abuse do to a loving, compassionate human being. This is what happens when one person refuses to take any responsibility for their actions, while the other is willing to absorb all of the blame if it means keeping the peace.

Making Big Decisions

One of the most humbling aspects about working in abuse recovery is that I can't tell anyone how to heal. Remember when you were a kid, your parents would give you a bunch of life lessons about how not to repeat their mistakes? Of course you ignored them, because no one can tell you how to be happy; you had to go off and make those very same mistakes yourself.

The stages of grief are exactly the same, but I still want to share some advice on the off chance that it happens to resonate with you.

During the denial phase, you should avoid making big, life-changing decisions. You will invest your happiness in so many different things, unable to realize that happiness must come from within. You will enthusiastically rip apart your life, confident that every idea you come up with is the next best solution.

But there is no solution.

There is nothing wrong with your job. There is nothing wrong with your salary. There is nothing wrong with your home, your phone, your profile picture, or your single status. None of these things is the problem. (You've been long trained to ignore the real problem.)

So in this stage, I strongly urge you to avoid making big decisions—especially ones involving money and friends. For now, you should *not* trust your gut instincts. Rarely will you ever hear me say that, but right now everything is out of balance. Your intuition is skewed, completely unhinged by the psychopath's abuse.

You will have plenty of time to sort out the friendship situation after you've gone through recovery. If you are suspicious of toxic friends, simply distance yourself from them for the time being. It does not need to be personal or unpleasant. Just tell them you're going through a difficult time, and you'll reconnect with them when you've found some peace. Then you will be free to dedicate some time to recovery forums where you know people will understand what you're going through. Your old friends will not get it, but this does not necessarily make them bad people. They will simply suggest that you "move on," giving you the best breakup advice they know. Ask yourself: If you hadn't gone through this experience, would you know how to empathize with a survivor?

If, in one year, you still want that new job, or want to send a nasty letter to a longtime friend, then go ahead and do it. But for now, your future self might be very grateful for your present self's patience.

Education and Self-Doubt

Symptoms: uncertainty, anxiety, curiosity, disbelief, excessive storytelling, self-blame, contradicting yourself.

This is where things start to change really fast. Somehow, you come across the topic of psychopathy or narcissism or sociopathy. Whether it be through a lucky Internet search, some prior life knowledge you picked up, or a skilled therapist, you now have the biggest piece of the puzzle. This is why the label matters. From here, everything starts to fall into place.

You know deep down that something within you is horribly broken. Even though you impatiently want to feel good again, you also want to figure out what in the world just happened. When you begin to read through the list of red flags of psychopathy, you will experience extreme self-doubt. You will recognize most—if not all—of the warning signs, but you will wonder if you're just labeling your ex a psychopath because you can't handle the truth of how you ruined the relationship. This is, of course, *the psychopath's* truth.

So you oscillate back and forth as you think about your idealizer and your abuser. How could someone who thought you were perfect be the very same person who intentionally hurt you? How could they go from obsession to contempt in the blink of an eye? It isn't possible. There's no way you dated a psychopath. They loved you. Right?

Cognitive Dissonance

What I've just described is a psychological phenomenon known as cognitive dissonance. It's a state of mind where your intuition is telling you two competing things. It's totally natural after a psychopathic relationship, because you're used to repeatedly being told things—instead of seeing them with your own two eyes, or feeling them in your heart. You constantly heard the psychopath make sweeping declarations of love and devotion, but you never actually felt them. You fondly remember the dreams you shared with them, and the future you planned together—but obviously those things didn't happen.

So what do you believe? Their actions or their words? During the relationship, you probably spent a lot of time with their words. Cherishing them, idolizing them, analyzing them, and ultimately distrusting them. But despite your intuition telling you something was wrong, a part of you still desperately wanted to believe in the manufactured soul mate.

And now you're dispelling these illusions. You don't fully understand how their mind works, but you know something wasn't quite right. So there's going to be a battle going on in your own mind—a battle to quell the dream of love and passion so that you have a chance to see things rationally.

You will switch from one extreme to the other. First, they're a total monster who cheated and lied throughout the relationship. Then they're really not the worst person in the world; they were just insensitive, and definitely didn't hurt you intentionally. If you forgive them, then maybe everyone could be happy. But wait, some of those things they said to you were really cruel. They made you feel like garbage, patronizing you as if you were a child. Then again, everyone deserves a second chance—you've always been taught not to hold grudges, and it'd be a lot more pleasant to remain friends with them. Plus, how could you forget those beautiful memories where you held hands as they said "I love you . . ."

And that's the danger of cognitive dissonance. It brings you back to the addictive love memories. It causes you to long for a broken dream, a manufactured lie. As you begin to work through these feelings, the diametrically opposed thoughts will become less and less extreme. But in the meantime, you are still very susceptible to their ongoing abuse. As long as you're experiencing cognitive dissonance, make no mistake: they will be able to trick you again. All it takes is one sweet word to send you right back to the idealization phase. So how can you protect yourself?

Two Masks

Delayed arrogance is common in sociopaths. When you first meet, they'll seem unusually innocent, humble, childlike, and thoughtful. But as time goes by, they inevitably transform into a monster: manipulative, arrogant, and neglectful. Whenever they are grooming new targets, they're on their best behavior, hooking others with babylike charm. The reason for this is that most people aren't attracted to blatant arrogance, and so sociopaths develop this vulnerable, "cute" persona in order to sink their claws in. But once the target is hooked, their true colors come to light. At their core, sociopaths are smug, patronizing, and narcissistic. Because of these two opposing masks, targets will go through great lengths to reconcile this monster with the childish sweetheart they remember. Targets also deal with a considerable amount of victim blaming, where they are accused of being attracted to jerks, or told "it takes two to tango." It does not take two to tango when one person uses a completely manufactured identity to convince another person that they are alike in every way.

No Contact

After a relationship with a psychopath, the No Contact rule is the only way to stay safe from their manipulation and abuse. There are no exceptions to this rule. No matter how badly you were hurt, contact will only make it worse. If you have children or other lasting connections to the psychopath, engage in the minimal amount of contact possible.

Cutting contact with toxic people will transform your life. At first, it feels miserable—like you're going cold turkey from an addiction. But as time goes on, you come to discover that each passing day brings unexpected new blessings. You begin to develop self-respect, boundaries, and true friendships. Instead of running around absorbing and forgiving everything, you spend time with people who do not behave in a way that requires constant explaining. This freedom allows your spirit to thrive. Someday you will look back and wonder how you even tolerated interacting with such unhealthy people. Your new self begins to feel protective of your old self, and that's a pretty neat place to be!

No Contact is exactly what it sounds like. It means you don't contact the psychopath in any way, shape, or form. So what constitutes contact? More than you might think.

Phone calls
Text messages
Seeing them in person
Emails
Facebook friendship
Facebook messages
Cyberstalking

Nothing good can come from contact with a psychopath, no matter how seemingly insignificant the contact might be. It will greatly hinder your healing process and you will always regret it later. Every bit of communication with the psychopath only serves to hurt you. They're always interested in triangulating you, but this can easily be mistaken for genuine care and interest. Given the chance, they will suck you back in with charm, only to resume the nightmare you remembered from the identity erosion. They will restore the idealization phase, triggering your return to cognitive dissonance. They will lie pathologically, driving you out of your mind. They will engage in word salad, uprooting your entire healing process. As soon as they get their claws into you again, you will be dragged back into their manipulative world. You must break free of this addiction—and the only way is through No Contact.

When your thoughts start to race and you're itching to make some contact with them, be aware of this. Find distractions for yourself. A new hobby, meditation, writing, work, a pet—anything to get your mind off the psychopath. The brain learns habits, so teach it healthier ones. When you notice your mind going back to the psychopath, take a deep breath and force yourself to think about other things.

The same goes for cyberstalking. Even though you're not directly communicating with them, you're still indulging an addiction. The only way to break that addiction is to cut off every channel with them, cold turkey. You can do it now by blocking them on Facebook, Twitter, and your cell phone.

You may think you'll feel better if you stick around to see their next target get dumped like you, but you won't. Nothing will change the pain you feel, except time and personal growth. Believe it or not, you will reach a period when you could not care less about what they are doing or whom they are courting.

Closure Without Contact

The following piece was written by my close friend and fellow administrator, HealingJourney. Her insights are amazing and I strongly encourage you to check out her book, *The Survivor's Quest: Recovery After Encountering Evil.*

All survivors of psychopathic evil know how extremely difficult it is to cut ties with a psychopath. And then once No Contact is established, survivors find themselves trying to pick up the pieces of their shattered hearts and lives. Many survivors write that what they want more than anything is to find closure. Some hope that they can somehow obtain that closure from the psychopaths. Others are convinced that closure is absolutely impossible. *All* survivors wonder, at some point during their recovery journeys, if they will ever find a way out of the darkness.

The good news is that *yes*, closure is possible. And no, it will *not* come from the psychopaths! It must come from *within*. The following are points on a possible path toward closure. This road map does not have a time line, and many of the points overlap:

TRY TO LET GO OF THE ILLUSION

The first step in healing from psychopathic abuse is to stop all contact with the psychopath. And the only way to do that is to let go of the image you had of the person you loved. Unfortunately and sadly, that person never existed. He or she was only an illusion, a mask the psychopath created in order to mirror and manipulate you. As crushingly hard as it is and as much as it hurts, the only way to find freedom is to stop believing in that illusion.

I clearly remember the beginning of the encounter I had with the psychopath; I thought he was the perfect partner for me! He seemed to understand me so well, and we had all the right things in common. It almost felt too good to be true! Then, when I discovered that he had so deeply betrayed me, in ways I never imagined were possible, I realized it *always was* too good to be true. All of it was a lie . . . except for *me* and my feelings for him. I was real, and my feelings were real. And in the midst of the intense pain, I held on to the light—the light of truth—that was just barely left in my soul. Letting go of the "dream man" he pretended to be brought me closer to my own heart.

So do your best to let go of the illusion. When you let go, you'll start to find the real you.

SEARCH FOR ANSWERS—BUT *STAY SAFE!*

When I realized that I had been involved with a pathological liar, I had a very strong urge to go on what I call "my truth-finding mission." Everyone around me—*absolutely everyone*—discouraged me from investigating the psychopath. But I felt deeply compelled to uncover as many lies as I could, so I disregarded their advice. It turned out that I made the right decision, because I conducted my mission *without making contact with the psychopath or anyone connected to him.* I also did not reveal my new knowledge to the psychopath or his fan club, although I desperately wanted to. Finally, when I exhausted every anonymous avenue available to me, I stopped. I was far from healed, and I uncovered only a portion of the truth, but I felt that I had reclaimed a part of myself. The entire process was an important step in rebuilding my self-respect.

It is completely okay to search for as many answers as you can, to uncover as much of the truth as possible, *as long as you follow the No Contact rule.*

RESEARCH PSYCHOPATHY

An encounter with a psychopath is not like a normal relationship, which means the aftermath is going to be very different from a typical breakup. Survivors are left with so many WHY questions, and those questions need to be answered in order for healing to occur. Survivors also tend to blame themselves for what happened, often because others do not understand what they have been through and usually make insensitive statements like "Why did you stay?" or "Why didn't you see the signs?" or "It takes two to tango."

But psychopaths are abnormal! At the time of the encounter, you did not know that such people existed. You were *innocent*. Be ready for others to discourage you from "focusing on them"—they might imply that it delays your recovery—but researching psychopathy actually helps you make much progress in your own healing. By learning to recognize the common tactics and games of psychopathic predators, you will realize that the abuse was never your fault. By learning how the psychopathic mind works, you will realize you were set up from the very beginning. And when it all begins to click for you, that is when you start to reclaim your power!

ALLOW YOURSELF TO FEEL AND THINK

All normal human beings attempt to avoid pain. Yet, paradoxically, it is by facing the pain and moving through it that we find beauty, because on the other side of our deepest suffering, we have the opportunity to experience the greatest joy. As you heal, you will find yourself moving back and forth through the stages of grief that are unique to the aftermath of an encounter with a psychopath. Allow yourself to feel all emotions as they come over you, which will most likely happen in waves. Also, allow the thoughts of the psychopath in when they overwhelm your mind, even though you may feel as if you are going crazy because you can think of nothing else. Continuously pushing the obsessive thoughts away can actually be more harmful than helpful. You most likely are experiencing symptoms of PTSD, and it is important to find resources that can help you work through the trauma of what has happened. This might include therapy and/or other healing techniques. Amazingly, if you step into the pain instead of running from it, you begin to see who you are at a deeper level. You develop self-respect and self-love and new confidence. You learn to trust your intuition. And when you are able to trust *yourself*, then you will start to find others who are worthy of your trust.

ACCEPT WHAT YOU CAN AND CANNOT CONTROL

When I learned the truth about the psychopath, I was extremely disturbed to realize that such evil exists in the world. The relationship was over, and I was deeply upset to see the psychopath move on to his new target, seemingly happy, not caring about the devastation he left behind him (me . . . broken me). My first reaction to this was complete heartbreak, shame, and outrage. I wanted to expose the psychopath for the monster he is. I wanted to convince the other person to leave him. I wanted him to apologize to me and actually mean it. I wanted justice, and I wanted revenge!

However, I knew that I could not stop him from lying to and manipulating and hurting others. I knew I could not convince his new target of the truth. And I knew I could not make him feel remorse for what he did to me. What I *could* do was focus on my own healing and my own life. When I made the choice to do that, one day at a time, I gradually felt happier and more peaceful. I still wage a daily war to relinquish the desire to control what I cannot control, but, thankfully, it is not nearly as difficult as it used to be. You will never receive traditional "closure" from the psychopath. But the light you can discover within your own soul is *so* much better!

TRUST IN YOUR OWN UNIQUE TRUTH

Perhaps the most significant epiphany during my recovery came when I finally was able to believe in myself and trust in my own truth. Psychopaths are eerily similar in so many ways, and yet many of the details of my encounter seemed so different from other survivors' stories. As I struggled to make sense out of what had happened to me, I heard so many opinions from so many people about how to heal, about who I was, about who I should be, about what to believe. I questioned myself, as I had always done, and as long as my intense self-doubt remained, my pain lingered. Ironically, it was only after reading survivor story after survivor story, so similar to mine and yet so different, that the fog began to lift. Only after reading so many other stories, and only after seeing my own worth, was I able to see the truth in my experience. I still have doubts, about so many things, but now I put them in perspective and listen first to the voice within my heart.

You have a similar voice in your own heart. Listen to it.

And please hold on to this truth: you *can* find closure without contact, and you *can* find peace on the other side of the nightmare. Read and learn about psychopathy, move through the pain, take back your power, and most of all, strive daily to believe in and love yourself, *your most authentic self. You* are your own best guide.

Un-Brainwashing

CONTRIBUTED BY SEARCHINGFORSUNSHINE

I've written this especially for all the people who are struggling to reach the point of No Contact, and to maintain it. I know those early days of No Contact are pure hell, and while what works for me may not work for everyone, I hope there is something here that can be of help to someone.

Where you probably find yourself in the early days of No Contact: You've discovered what the word "psychopath" really means, for the first time, ever. In your desperation for answers about the toxic relationship you're caught up in, you do some Googling. You type in the catchphrase that leads you to an article about psychopaths, narcissists, or sociopaths. Maybe you've even typed in the catchphrase that leads you to Psychopath Free. You cannot believe it, because the people you're reading about sound just like the person you're involved with. The words resonate completely in your gut. Your mind even understands perfectly what has just happened to you. You have "aha" moments in rapid succession. You can't believe you've finally found the answers. You're ready to end it, right now.

To your horror, not long after reaching this decision (whether you've acted on it yet or not), you suddenly begin doubting yourself. "What if they aren't? . . . maybe, just maybe, it's me . . . maybe I'm imagining that they're a psychopath, they did say that I'm needy . . ." You Google that article you found, again. You read it again. You get a few more of those "aha" moments you got the first time you read it. Another few things fall into place. "Yes, it's them, it's not me!" you think. They're a psychopath/sociopath, you know it for sure now. More realizations are clicking into place for you. You can see why they said the contradictory things that they said. You are remembering exact phrases they uttered, exact scenarios, and seeing them all in a new light. Yet, once again, you fall back down the hole of self-doubt. Once again, you find your-self wondering, "Is it me? Am I absolutely sure it's not me?"

Why the cognitive dissonance tears us to shreds: What I've de-scribed above is what cognitive dissonance feels like—this is what it feels like to you, and how it felt to me, in my desperation to come to grips with what happened to me. You only feel this way because you were brainwashed into believing you were the dysfunctional party in the relationship. You were provoked by your partner's lies/betrayal/broken promises into reacting, as anyone would be. They used that against you, to ensure that you believe it's all your fault, to ensure they retain power over you. This makes you want to "give it one last try," because feeling that it's all your fault gives you control over the situation in that you believe that if you behave differently, they will become loving toward you again.

All of your thoughts about it being your fault are totally untrue. Only you can't see this clearly because you've had lies about who you are and your part in this relationship pounded into your brain, over and over again. This creates cognitive dissonance, causing you to have doubts about ending it. Compounding this is the fact that in the initial phase of the relationship, they did an excellent job of idealizing and love-bombing you. The vicious circle then comes in to play, in that you cannot see clearly who they are and the cognitive dissonance won't leave you until you've done some No Contact time. But it's hard to feel at peace with your decision to go No Contact while the cognitive dissonance is wreaking havoc in your mind.

What worked for me to end the cognitive dissonance: Well, I went through utter hell inside this mental tug-of-war for the first six weeks of No Contact. Yet every single time I read the material available on psychopaths, narcissists, and sociopaths, all of my cognitive dissonance vanished. This was because my gut, my instinct, was recognizing the truth that it wasn't me, that he was indeed a psychopath. The information I read resonated with such utter truth within my soul that even my confused mind couldn't override and overshadow it. I realized that I needed to have more of those moments of clarity; I began to see how I had been brainwashed; I began to realize that I had experienced those moments of my gut instinct speaking to me before, just a few weeks into the relationship. So I realized the only way I was going to get through this was to tell my mind to shut up when that torturous tug-of-war cognitive dissonance began again.

I resolved to read the material describing psychopathic behaviors each time I had the need to tell my mind to be quiet. I understood that the way to healing and to getting my mind to grasp the truth was to have fewer questions running through my mind, and more truths resonating from deep within my soul—more of those "aha" moments . . . In those early days, I also stayed away from all the triggers—places, music, and people—that reminded me of the relationship, and/or invalidated my experience as a victim/survivor of a relationship with a psychopath.

This is exactly how I maintained No Contact, and shut up once and for all the doubting voice screaming at me through the cognitive dissonance, which before had never seemed to run out of ideas with which to challenge me.

What I'm saying is, there comes a time in your recovery process when all the answers to all the questions you are asking are just going to lead to more questions. There comes a time when the endless analysis needs to stop, a time when you have to learn to quiet your brain and learn to listen to your gut and accept what it is telling you. If you keep filling your brain with doubts because of the psychopath's lies, and reaffirming them, you won't leave any space inside your mind for the truth.

Your mind needs to be washed with, and awash in, the truth. The percentage of truth you put into your mind is in direct proportion to the percentage of psychopathic brainwashing that you put out of it. To put it simply, as the truth grows larger, the psychopath's brainwashing will grow smaller. The more your brain is washed in the truth, the more the lies that the psychopath pounded into your brain recede and eventually fade away. Then, finally, one morning you will wake up and realize that the truth has found its way into your mind; it's slowly filtered up from your gut, to replace all the lies the psychopath told you. There is inner peace, at last.

Hopefully, this section has provided you with some useful tools to jump-start your journey. Disseminating the truth is the best way to help yourself out of the dark. Knowledge is power to survivors, and poison to psychopaths. The more information you have, the better. And once it all begins to sink in—well, then you're really in for something.

Please see the Resources section at the back of this book for articles, books, and videos that can educate you and help you fight cognitive dissonance.

The Stages of Grief—Part II

You found the missing puzzle piece—the word that changes everything. You discovered psychopathy. And from here on out, everything starts to fall into place. Suddenly you have words to describe what happened to you. Every inexplicable memory can now be explained, which leads to a lot of strange, new emotions. It'll feel unpleasant at first, but that's because you're recovering from something unpleasant. You'll question yourself a lot, and that's a good thing. Questioning yourself (and the world around you) is the start to a long path of introspection that will forever alter the course of your life.

Understanding the Psychopath

Symptoms: physical sickness, need for validation, shock, disgust, "aha" moments, paranoia, sinking feeling in your chest.

This is one of the strangest and most important stages in the healing process. Education can only take you so far. To really understand the psychopath, you need to actually feel what they feel. Most victims live by the values of compassion and love, so it's nearly impossible to imagine empathizing with a psychopath. In fact, this is why they're able to get away with so much—because normal human beings automatically project their consciences onto everyone else.

As you delve deeper into your research, you will inadvertently lose a bit of yourself. You will become so consumed by psychopathy that you'll actually begin to understand how the psychopath's mind works. You'll recognize not just the red flags and verbal abuse, but the sadistic pleasure they felt when they destroyed you, the silence—even laughter—that you received when you were begging and crying. Instead of excusing everything as insensitive or dense, you look back on the relationship and view all of their behavior from a very different perspective.

And suddenly everything clicks.

It all makes sense, when it never did before. From the mirroring to the love-bombing to the identity erosion to the triangulation to the eventual abandonment. You feel disgusted. You realize you were never loved—just another target in a never-ending cycle. You start to see that you've never behaved like this in any other relationship, and it wasn't because they were special. It was because they were actively working against you from the moment they chose you.

You look back at all of the things that once made you feel paranoid, now able to see that every instance of abuse and neglect was calculated and intentional. And finally, you come to the horrifying realization that the love of your life—the person you trusted with all your heart—set you up for failure since the very beginning.

The Robot

Because they have no identity of their own, the psychopath is able to become exactly what their target seeks in a romantic partner. You will notice a short "observation" period, during which they enthusiastically declare how similar you both are. During this time, they are simply listening to you describe your hopes and dreams, and then producing an exaggerated mirror image of everything you've shared with them. They use this manufactured "connection" to build immediate trust, quickly leading you to believe that you've found your perfect soul mate. They appear to be fascinated with you on every level, texting you on a minute-by-minute basis and posting all over your Facebook profile for your friends to see. This person begins to consume your entire life, and suddenly you can't imagine how you were ever happy without them. But then the triangulation begins. And this is where the predator's lack of identity is most clearly evinced. They start to lure in denounced former lovers and potential future mates with ambiguous hints and inside jokes, subtly ensuring that you see it all. You begin to feel like you're playing detective, when actually the clues are being spoon-fed to you. These hints make you feel jealous and crazy as you watch your soul mate openly idealize other targets. But the strangest thing of all is that the psychopath's persona changes drastically in order to match these new targets. You find them flattering things they once insulted, laughing at jokes that aren't funny, and transforming their entire personality to become somebody you don't even recognize. If you point out the fact that something has changed, you will be deemed "crazy" or "hypersensitive." And perhaps most unsettling of all, they often steal a little bit of your personality to use during the grooming process with their next victim. Like a sophisticated robot, they evolve and improve with every target, borrowing the traits that work and disposing of the depleted remains.

Intention and Sadism

One of the greatest myths surrounding psychopaths is this Hollywood pseudo psychology that psychopaths are actually victims themselves. Whether it be an abusive past, an absent father, or something in between—the idea is that psychopaths cannot help their behavior.

I don't agree with this at all.

Unlike people with other mental disorders, psychopaths are keenly aware of the impact that their behavior has on others. That's half the fun for them—watching people suffer. They pick up on insecurities and vulnerabilities in a heartbeat, and then make the conscious choice to exploit those qualities. They know the difference between right and wrong, and simply choose to steamroll straight through it.

The psychopathic relationship cycle is not some accidental by-product of insensitivity and emotional "thickness." It is a calculated, personalized process that psychopaths use to methodically torture their victims. Imagine the time and planning that go into mirroring someone else's hopes and dreams. The psychopath spends months—sometimes years—playing the role of a completely different person. All for one end: your destruction. They did not feel even a small amount of love for you, even when they claimed you were the only one who ever made them feel this way. No, the entire time they were just closely observing you, patiently waiting for the fun to start. Did you notice that as soon as you fell in love and became comfortable in the relationship, that's when the emotional abuse started? From there, you spent the rest of the relationship frantically trying to revitalize the soul mate they once pretended to be.

The problem is, many survivors equate the psychopath's insatiable drive for attention with some sort of childlike insecurity. But they're not insecure. They love themselves. They love the way they look, the way they can trick everyone around them, and the way their victims beg for them. When you are in a relationship with a psychopath, you are not filling some sort of void within their broken soul. They have no soul. They want to be worshiped and nothing else. They're not a lost little boy or girl hiding behind a tough persona, their disorder is not a defense mechanism for deep-seated fragilities. You're never going to find a "soft spot" within them. Just endless darkness.

At some point, you must stop thinking along the lines of "I'll go No Contact because it'll take away their narcissistic supply." This implies that you still (or ever did) fill some sort of personal need within them. You don't, and you never will. They do not seek out attention from others in order to inflate their ego. It's already fully inflated, and I can assure you it'll never deflate.

They want your attention so that they can consume you and then destroy you. They saw you as disposable trash. And given the chance, they might recycle you, but it's never because they need you.

And what's more, your healing process should not revolve around giving or withholding attention from someone else. You should be going No Contact because you genuinely believe that you deserve better. This is someone who manipulated, lied, abused, and deeply hurt you. As you develop self-respect, you should come to understand that this is all more than enough reason to remove someone from your life—permanently.

Am I a Psychopath?

Too often, survivors come to the very disconcerting conclusion that *they* might be a psychopath. After months of studying the topic and thinking about the experience, I think it's only natural that you might begin to question yourself and your own good nature. It's a nasty topic, even addictive at times. When your mind constantly bounces back to psychopathy, it's normal that you apply your knowledge to nearly everyone in your life, including yourself.

I've come up with several reasons why you are probably not a psychopath, because the last thing you need during the healing process is some nagging doubt that you're evil. You don't need this worry—and that's the key word here: worry. Psychopaths would never worry about this. And moreover, they just don't care. You're scared because you see psychopathy as the root of all evil. But they don't see their disorder as the terrible sickness that it is. They see it as a strength. They believe their lack of conscience makes them superior. Do you think like that? I'm going to guess not. So here are the main reasons you're probably asking the question:

1. THE PSYCHOPATH MADE YOU FEEL THIS WAY

Throughout the relationship, the psychopath projects their flaws onto you. They call you needy, jealous, clingy, controlling, evil, and crazy, and you may start to believe you actually do act this way. But let me ask you this: Have you ever felt that way in any normal relationship or friendship? Do you feel that way around your Constant? No. So what is the common denominator here? The above behaviors are all characteristics of psychopathy, and you only exhibit them when you're around this person. And it's no coincidence that these traits slowly disappear as you spend more time away from them.

Victims tend to absorb all of the problems in a relationship, believing that they can forgive and understand everything in order to save the perfect idealization phase. When you do this, you end up absorbing many of the psychopath's most horrible flaws, causing you to believe that you actually have those traits. After the identity erosion and grand finale, it is only natural to feel disgusted with yourself and your behavior. But you haven't been yourself. You became a receptacle for the psychopath's poison. But with time and No Contact, you begin to see that you don't display any of those characteristics when you're not around them. In fact, you seem to become more gentle, empathetic, and compassionate—closer to your most genuine self. That is the real you.

2. YOUR PERSONALITY TYPE

There's this old saying that goes "Don't believe everything you think." This is extremely important to remember in the aftermath of the grand finale. Most survivors tend to share a variety of common personality traits, two of them being open-mindedness and susceptibility to suggestions. These two qualities are actually great strengths, but they can cause problems if you don't introspect a bit and learn to control them. The issue is, when you ask yourself, "Am I a psychopath?" your open mind will automatically entertain the idea. That's not because there's any rational reason to believe you're a psychopath, it's just because you have an open mind. That's it. When your mind suggests something to you, you listen. And sometimes you just need to teach yourself to laugh it off as the ridiculous notion that it is.

Unfortunately, many survivors also tend to be very open to suggestions that they themselves are awful—and closed off to suggestions that someone else might be awful. As you recover and begin to return to a saner place, you should stop seeing yourself in such a negative light and start recovering your perspective. This means you adopt more of an "I'm okay, you're okay" mentality instead of the toxic "I'm not okay, you're okay" that dominated most of your relationship. So just remember that you have an open mind and are likely to be much more susceptible to hypnosis and suggestions than other personality types. Be aware of this, and learn how to use it.

Along these lines, depression can also be coloring your view. During depression, negative thoughts find a way to stay in your mind by convincing your brain that they are more important than the positive thoughts. Just like a virus, depression develops survival mechanisms so that you remain depressed. It convinces you that your positive thoughts are just delusions and ignorance. But those negative thoughts running crazy in your mind are not real. Your brain is playing tricks on you. You are not a psychopath.

3. YOU HAVE BOUNDARIES

Abusers happily cheat, lie, verbally assault, manipulate, confuse, and ignore others, but survivors often find that when they try to react firmly and stand up to this abuse, they immediately end up feeling bad. Let go of this inner turmoil. Having boundaries is what makes you healthy. Intentionally and remorselessly harming someone else is what makes an abuser.

You are probably not accustomed to having boundaries. In fact, many survivors never had boundaries to begin with. A strange gift from the psychopathic experience is that you begin to find these boundaries. Some call it healthy narcissism, but I think "self-respect" is a better term. The problem is, boundaries and self-respect are completely foreign to you at this point. So when you begin to manifest these things, you feel like a selfish, abrasive jerk. When in reality, you've just stopped playing the role of a selfless doormat.

You may begin to find that old friendships and toxic dynamics fall apart as you become stronger. It almost feels as if you're being punished for healing. But that's not the case. You're actually finally strong enough to allow only what's healthy into your life. You're not psychopathic or narcissistic for having boundaries and expecting a decent level of respect in return. You're just a regular human being with feelings. But you may be surrounded by people who don't want you to be regular—they prefer the person who caters to their every need. So they make you feel bad for taking on healthier habits. This kind of conditioning can make you feel psychopathic and unempathetic, but again, that is not the case. It's what happens when selfish people stop getting their way. They fight for the status quo, because the existing dynamic suits them. But it doesn't suit you, and that's what boundaries help you realize. Just because you have to tell someone off or demand a bit of respect does not make you psychopathic. It makes you stronger. Every time you stand up for yourself, a part of your spirit comes back to life.

4. YOU EXPERIENCED THE RELATIONSHIP CYCLE FOR YOURSELF

Psychopathic relationships have a tried and true pattern: idealize, devalue, discard—every single time. But they're not the only one who cycles through that series. You experience phases, too. The difference is in the order. You idealize them, more than you have idealized anyone in your life. Then, you are discarded, left broken and alone to pick up pieces. And finally, you begin to devalue them as you learn about psychopathy. You deconstruct the person from the grooming phase, just like they deconstructed you during the identity erosion.

This is not a natural cycle for any person to go through after a breakup. Sure, plenty of exes end up disliking each other, but they don't go through such a roller coaster of highs and lows, deconstructing personality traits they once idealized. Unfortunately, the only way to heal is to go through this toxic cycle yourself. Only then will you finally manage to see that it was all false. An illusion. A perverted mirror. In order to do so, you must begin the unnatural process of undoing everything you once loved. Not just some of it. All of it. Because none of it was ever real. Only then can you find self-respect and reclaim your dreams.

Additionally, you will go through many other devaluing processes. Many survivors cyberstalk for a while, mainly because they have absolutely no idea what just happened. Social networking provides an opportunity to gain some more insight into the truth, but eventually you must realize that it is not helpful in your healing process. The bottom line is, cyberstalking counts as contact, and it doesn't do you any good. You probably got addicted to cyberstalking during the idealization phase, when you isolated yourself and waited desperately by the computer for their every update. They knew this and loved the power it gave them. But realize that they were doing the same thing as you, although they were probably much better at hiding it. For instance, they might have claimed that they barely ever checked your Facebook feed anymore, and then accidentally referenced something you posted a few days ago. Or they might have said they weren't expecting your call, when they were actually wondering what took you so long. So don't beat yourself up for getting caught up in the mind games. Just understand that this addiction is unhealthy, and that self-control can finally put an end to it.

During and after the psychopathic relationship, you've prob-ably done things you're not proud of—you've lied, sought atten-tion, and sent off angry emails. That doesn't make you a psychopath. At some point, you need to forgive yourself and make a conscious effort to start making better choices. You are not that nasty, stalking, mirroring, vengeful ex. It takes a lot of time and effort to purge your system of the toxic relationship cycle, but you can get there, and you can seek out normal, loving relationships.

5. YOUR EMPATHY IS COMPLETELY DESTABILIZED

You will feel empty and numb for long periods of time. That is the nature of psychopathic recovery. But numbness does not equal psychopathy. It means your emotions were trampled on and ma-nipulated, and it's going to take a long time for them to come back again. Yes, a psychopath is emotionally numb, but they are that way for life. They would never spend months mourning the loss of their own innocence or ruminating about their broken heart.

Your emotions and empathy are just in hibernation. And one day, the sleeping bear will wake up stronger than ever. When all is said and done, you will find yourself more perceptive and com-passionate than ever before. So don't worry about feeling numb right now. It goes away, and it's replaced by something much better.

Remember my recommendation that you wait several months before forming new friendships and relationships? The reason is that you'll feel frustrated and depressed because you can't seem to experience the same love or high that you had with the psy-chopath. You'll feel like a bad person for getting annoyed that your new partner doesn't seem to be as attentive and sensual. You can't keep getting caught up in these postpsychopathic relationships, because they only harm you and the people around you. You will be overwhelmed with guilt, on top of your already damaged empathy.

So instead of beating yourself up for being unable to accomplish the impossible, spend some time introspecting and becoming your own best friend. But even introspection has its limits—at some point you must stop thinking and start living. This might take years, but you will know in your heart when you're ready. Too much introspection can drive a person mad. But just the right amount can bring about all sorts of wisdom and creativity

6. YOU HAVE A HEIGHTENED UNDERSTANDING OF EVIL

A lot of survivors once walked through this world believing that all people had some amount of good in them. The psychopath served as a nasty wake-up call from that blissful ignorance. As you learn more about psychopathy, you also learn more about human nature. You understand how and why the psychopath tricked you—how they played on your greatest insecurities. How they love-bombed you. How they set off a chemical addiction.

And then, suddenly, you might feel a little bit dark inside. It's like you've come too close to evil. And now you know how you could flatter someone into doing anything for you. Or how you could make someone feel suicidal. It's some really nasty knowledge that you'd probably prefer not to have. But think about it, would you ever act on it? Of course not. Your conscience would stop you in a heartbeat. That's what separates you from the psychopaths. Not the knowledge, but your conscience and resulting actions. So no, you are not evil for having this new understanding of people and the world.

J. K. Rowling wrote: "We've all got both light and dark inside us. What matters is the part we choose to act on. That's who we really are." Keep that in mind during your healing process. Every person has their own demons—what defines us is how we choose to handle them.

Recall the blissful days when you knew nothing about psychopathy. Life was good. Did you ever feel evil for enjoying a compliment? Manipulative for being kind? Ill-intentioned for doing a good deed? My guess is no. It's only when you encountered something so sinister that you began to question yourself. Well, enough already. You are not a psychopath, and you never were. Like everything else, the soul heals and you will find your equilibrium again as your empathy and emotions come back to life.

You've been conditioned to see compliments and attention as some sort of weapon, but they're not. Appreciating a compliment or enjoying some attention every now and then does not make you a psychopath. You need to feel comfortable accepting these things from normal, healthy people. Don't let your understanding of how you were manipulated stop you from enjoying one of the nicest things in life: positive energy.

You are not a psychopath. You're the polar opposite. And that's the only reason you're asking this question in the first place.

Delayed Emotions

Symptoms: rage, depression, extreme jealousy, racing thoughts, hatred, overwhelming temptation to contact the abuser.

Once you understand the psychopath, you're going to experience a lot of unpleasant emotions. So get comfortable, because you're going to be here for a while.

In this stage, you will begin to feel all of the things you weren't allowed to feel during the relationship. Remember the emotions you brushed aside in order to maintain peace with them? Those didn't actually go anywhere—they just stirred around in your heart for a while, manifesting as self-doubt and anxiety. But now that you finally understand how the psychopath's games work, you're absolutely sickened. You feel tricked. Manipulated. Violated.

Rage

Your self-doubt is replaced by anger. You know the truth. You see how you were used, groomed, and brainwashed. You're beyond angry. You want to murder them. You want to contact everyone in their life and tell them what they did. You want to write them a letter and tell them to burn in hell. You obsessively talk about it with your friends and family—you need to get your story out there. You've been shut up and minimized for so long, and now your voice is finally free.

Whenever you accused them of cheating or lying, they would turn it around and blame it on you, so you felt bad instead of mad. This cognitive dissonance caused a huge suppression of anger, but it is finally coming out now. You may also feel the delayed emotion of jealousy as you realize how long the cheating was going on—how they used your manufactured behavior to court someone else with sympathy and pity. The smear campaign makes you feel the need to prove and defend yourself.

This delayed rage is completely expected after a psychopathic relationship. It can take months, even years, to feel. Please, if possible, do not act on it. No good can come from it. The greatest thing you can do is to remain calm and composed. The psychopath wants you to feel rage so they can show everyone how crazy you are—and how much you still love them. They will use you for triangulation long after the relationship has ended, even when you go No Contact.

And what's more, anger can only take you so far. It's an essential part of the healing process, but it won't bring you any long-term peace. Its main purpose on the healing journey is to develop your self-respect—an understanding that you deserved so much better.

Depression

You will swing back and forth between depression and rage for a very long time. You'll have good days and bad days, unable to maintain any sort of consistency in your moods. One night, you will think you're ready to move on; the next morning, you'll wake up crying and screaming into a pillow.

You don't want to be sad. And you don't deserve to be mad. All you did was fall in love. Why are you being punished for falling in love?

You find it impossible to go anywhere without thinking about your abuser. Every couple you come across reminds you of your lost relationship. Your old love songs seem to come up on the radio every second of the day. You can't even have a glass of wine without bursting into tears and embarrassing yourself.

And so you begin to isolate yourself from the world around you, surrounding yourself with people who understand you on discussion forums. You have obsessive, racing thoughts. The tiniest things set you off. Your boundaries are returning—or perhaps being formed for the very first time—and you can't believe you let yourself sink so low. Only now are you beginning to realize how much you truly lost. How much you uprooted in your own life to make room for this evil person. Not just friends, money, and life experiences—but also your happiness. Your kind understanding of the world has been shattered. Instead of giving people the benefit of the doubt, you suddenly have trouble trusting.

You begin to notice a constant feeling of dread and tightness in your chest—the demon that wraps its claws around your heart, always there to remind you of everything you want to forget.

When Empathetic People Self-Destruct

I believe that most empathetic people have a "self-destruct" mode. This often happens when all of our efforts to maintain the relationship finally come crashing down, and we realize that no matter how hard we tried, it was never enough. Once we slip into that self-destructive mode, we go through a few phases:

1. OVERDRIVE

In this phase you are desperately trying to empathize with everything and everyone around you. You're reaching out to new people, attempting to give them exactly what you think they might need, and hoping for love and appreciation in return. You're spending inordinate amounts of time and energy on people in need. During this period, you might find yourself agreeing with things you don't truly agree with, and making a lot of connections with people that you will later regret. You are on a mission to prove that empathy can improve any situation or person.

2. ANGER

At this point, you may still be denying the fact that you've surrounded yourself with people who are insatiable. Realizing that none of your efforts are working, you become furious and declare war against your past self, against everything you once stood for. No more Mr. Nice Guy/Gal. No more doormat. You overcompensate by becoming somewhat abrasive, and often lose friends in the process.

3. LONELINESS

In every dreamer's journey, there is going to be a long period of quiet and solitude. This is uncomfortable at first, especially after you have become accustomed to seeking the approval of others in order to feel a sense of self-worth. But eventually, this alone time actually becomes quite pleasant. Without so much feedback, you finally have a chance to focus on some pressing internal struggles. With no one's judgments but our own, we have this great opportunity to discover who we truly are. It is during this alone time that we begin to rebuild our identity from scratch, after being wiped out by whatever darkness we encountered.

4. BALANCE

You start to discover that there is a healthy equilibrium some-where in sections 1, 2, and 3 above. You do not need to empathize with everyone around you. Empathy is something to be saved for people you trust and care about—people who are capable of re-ciprocating it. You also do not need to put on a tough persona in order to avoid being a doormat. You can demonstrate your self-respect simply by living it. And finally, you do not need to shut yourself off from the world to avoid being hurt. There are so many good people out there, and once you have properly self-destructed, you will be ready to take part in this magical world again. With a healthy balance, your qualities become gifts that will stay with you for as long as you live.

Some of us have spent years, even decades, without hitting the self-destruct button. Once we do, at first it feels very volatile and upsetting. But ultimately, empathetic people need to go through this journey. This is how we begin to form boundaries, and it's how we learn to love the world again—this time with a little wis-dom to go along with our wonder.

Exposing a Psychopath: Should You Warn the Next Victim?

We've all been there. Through a lucky Google search, you came across your first few articles about psychopathy and everything started to fall into place. It's uncanny, overwhelming, infuriating, horrifying, and a lot of other awful emotions.

For many of us, our first reactions are:

1. Expose the psychopath.
2. Warn the next victim.

It's so tempting to take some triggering words from an article you just discovered and send it to your ex and their next victim in an impulsive email, proving that you know exactly what they are.

Here is the assumption: The psychopath will be scared that you know what they are, finally wiping that superior smirk off their face. The next target will read your letter and recognize all of the red flags and dump the psychopath immediately. You'll become best of friends and have coffee together every day.

Here is the typical reality: The psychopath will use your words to prove to the world how obsessed, bitter, and crazy you are. You have to keep in mind that very few people know or care about psychopathy. So instead, they'll see someone who's still in love and can't handle rejection. Your frantic messages will be used to triangulate the new target, making them feel even more special and desired, using your "craziness" as a bonding mechanism.

Your message to the new target will fall on deaf ears. When you were being love-bombed and idealized, would you have been swayed by a message calling your soul mate a psychopath?

If you've already done these things, don't worry about it. Life goes on, and in some cases it actually does work out fine. I'm sure in retrospect, when the new target is on the other side, left destroyed by the psychopath, he or she will appreciate that you tried to warn them. Either way, there is no shame in feeling that overwhelming need for revenge, especially after what happened to you.

But you deserve to be happy, and happiness starts with No Contact. Your heart needs a lot of time and love to start healing, but that can't happen when your energy is focused on deconstructing an extremely toxic dynamic.

Share your story, vent all you need, write out unsent letters—these are all essential parts of the process. As thousands of forum members will tell you, it gets so much better, and there will come a time when you just could not care less about the new relationship. As days become weeks, and weeks become months, you'll completely forget about how long it's been and start living life for *you*. That is what this journey is about. Cultivating self-respect, gentleness, and happiness.

Complex PTSD

Symptoms: numbness, feeling of disconnect, flashbacks, triggering memories, aversion to love and sex, two "yous," isolation.

Once you've felt all the emotions you needed to feel, your spirit will be left broken, exhausted. Because when all is said and done, you know you can't remain angry and depressed forever. There comes a point when it's no longer healthy venting—just addictive rumination. You know you'll never get back together with this abusive person, and you understand that you cannot change the past.

So what comes next? How do you go back to your daily life, learning to cope with the abuse you suffered? How do you enjoy each day without the excessive flattery and approval that you'd grown so accustomed to? Something about the world just seems different now. Lifeless. Dull. Hopeless.

You find that the most obscure triggers set you off, unable to enjoy a date or some time with an old friend. You're on high alert the entire time, constantly looking out for manipulation and red flags. The slightest jokes will offend you. That feeling of dread in your heart never seems to go away—warning you that anyone and everyone could be out to hurt you.

And then, after you spend time with others, you overanalyze the experience and come up with a list of reasons that this person shouldn't be in your life anymore. Then you feel awful for thinking those things, guilty and ashamed that you could be so disloyal. Your opinions of others will oscillate between positive and negative, just like they did for the psychopath. You are now applying the horror you experienced to every aspect of your life, even though the psychopath has been gone for quite some time.

Contrary to popular belief, you do not need to be a war veteran or a kidnap victim to suffer from PTSD. Your current situation fits every one of the criteria for this disorder:

1. **Exposure to a traumatic event.** Yes, relationship abuse from someone you love is traumatic and life-altering.

2. **Persistent reexperiencing.** Yes, through the "mean and sweet" cycle, you were repeatedly subjected to their abuse.

3. **Persistent avoidance and emotional numbing.** Yes, this is the coping mechanism you adopted to excuse their behavior.

4. **Persistent symptoms of increased arousal not present before.** Yes, you begin to feel these during the delayed emotions stage, ultimately manifesting as anxiety and fear.

5. **Duration of symptoms for more than one month.** Yes, most survivors will require anywhere from twelve to twenty-four months of recovery before they begin to trust and love again.

6. **Significant impairment.** You tell me—how do you feel right about now? I'd say "impaired" is an understatement.

As you come to understand that your brain chemicals were altered by this experience, you should feel comfortable seeking out professional help from those who know how to combat this debilitating obstacle in the healing process. There is no shame in mental illness—all you need to worry about is finding the right help for you. I personally had a great experience working with a therapist who specialized in relationship abuse. My time with her was life-changing, and she's responsible for so much of the peace I feel now. Keep in mind, just like anything else, there are also bad "professionals" out there. If you do choose to speak with someone, remember you have every right to like or dislike them. There are going to be so many professionals to choose from, so do not settle for someone unless you feel 100 percent satisfied. Trust your intuition when it comes to finding the perfect match.

Truth Triumphs

Those who have encountered a psychopath, sociopath, or narcissist often feel as if they have been touched by pure evil—haunted by a constant anxiety, self-doubt, and lingering darkness that can't quite be explained. It feels as if your life force has been drained away, and you become numb to the things that once made you happy. People without conscience have this effect on empathetic beings— the reaction between soulful and soulless is life-altering. Ultimately, it becomes one of the most important experiences you could imagine. You begin to see the world as it truly is, and yourself as you truly are. Your energy slowly returns, and because your spirit generates this power from within, it cannot be broken.

Do-Over

One of the most common feelings associated with PTSD is powerlessness. Both during and after the abuse, you come to feel powerless to change your situation in any way. You realize that you were charmed, duped, used, and discarded—and there was absolutely nothing you could have done to avoid it. Just when you thought you'd hit rock bottom, the psychopath came along and took away what little remaining dignity you had. They made sure your behavior was as hysterical and embarrassing as possible. And no matter how terribly they treated you, it always felt like they were "winning" (I'll go into this in much more detail later on in the book).

Once you realize this was all a game to the other person, this powerlessness begins to feel even more overwhelming. You look back at every instance when you were begging and pleading, now aware that they were silently enjoying your reactions. You recall each time they called you crazy and jealous, now aware that you were right all along—they *were* actively cheating on you. You think to yourself, "If only they would contact me one more time, that way *I* could be the one to ignore them."

This is called a do-over, and I think it's your spirit's way of healing from a completely powerless situation. Your imagination is an incredibly powerful tool that wants nothing more than to make sure your heart stops hurting. So allow yourself to dream up these do-overs when the bad memories won't leave you alone. Sure, the annoying part of your brain might try to remind you that none of it is "real," but imagination is every bit as real as we decide it is.

Instead of begging and pleading, maybe you laughed at their nasty criticisms. Instead of apologizing profusely, maybe you found yourself demanding an apology. Instead of crying when they gave you the silent treatment, maybe you gave that silence right back to them. Instead of being dumped in the most insensitive way imaginable, maybe you were the one to walk out the door and never speak to them again.

Basically, you undo all of the parts in which they brought you to your knees. You do not allow them the satisfaction of calmly watching while you frantically scramble around for them. Instead, with your newfound knowledge of psychopathy, you become the calm one and beat them at all of their own games.

Not only is this natural after an abusive relationship, I think it's actually much healthier than reliving the same trauma over and over again. You used your imagination to absorb their abuse and romanticize nonexistent good qualities in them during the devaluation. So why in the world shouldn't you be allowed to use that same imagination to work through all of this pain?

With time, you'll come to see that the frantic, broken, anxious, unhinged version of you was nothing to be ashamed of. You were simply a kindhearted person reacting to a very unkind situation. Those outbursts and behaviors were the result of your most admirable qualities being exploited and eroded. It took me quite some time to come to this conclusion, but when I look back on my old mess of a self, I actually feel a strange sort of admiration for that person. He was doing everything he could with an impossible situation, and I will always respect him for that.

Of course, a part of me would like to go back in time and save him from it all—but I don't think that do-over would be particularly helpful to either of us.

New Pain After the Darkness

After the psychopathic experience, life seems to stand still for a while. You pour all of your energy into research, validation, and healing. The world around you stops while you work to regain a sense of self. But inevitably, life goes on. And such being the case, painful things continue to happen. Whether it be death of a friend or family member, another breakup, loss of a beloved pet, an illness, or anything else, you will experience pain. But after the psychopath, it's different. You find yourself always going back to this: "I could have coped with this so much better if that psychopath thing had never happened."

You burden yourself with more misery, finding that each challenge seems to lead you back to the toxic relationship, even if it's totally unrelated.

This is especially true for breakups, where you had a glimmer of hope and joy with someone else—an experience that finally made you forget about the psychopath. And once that's gone, the feelings come rushing back, like a second wave of the identity erosion, even though the psychopath is long gone.

I don't believe these feelings actually have anything to do with the psychopath. Your spirit has transformed, becoming more sensitive and vulnerable to sadness. You might initially interpret this as a bad thing, because it makes you feel weak when you need strength the most.

But this negative energy you're feeling has a bigger and more important purpose. Instead of digging through old memories, allow yourself to let go. Cry as much as you want to. Send out waves of loving energy, to heal where it is needed, or to touch what is already gone. You will find yourself exhausted, but also at peace, connected to something deeper than yourself.

Dealing with grief will never be the same again, but that doesn't have to be a bad thing. It only feels bad at first because you have no idea where to direct all of these new and overwhelming emotions. So you go back to what feels familiar—when you felt the absolute worst. But you soon learn ways to deal with pain-ful emotions and direct them in a more healthy way.

Here's another thing to keep in mind when you're feeling down: How many other things have become easier to cope with because of this whole experience? Most survivors find better friendships, healthier relationships, self-respect, boundaries, and a broader connection with humanity.

Negativity can work like a rolling snowball sometimes, and it's important to remember how far you've come. Give yourself some credit for pulling yourself out from the ashes.

You survived the darkness. You do not need to fear it anymore.

Embarrassment

After making it through the early, ugly stages of grief, many vic-tims feel ashamed of themselves and the relationship aftermath. They cannot believe they sank so low, actually begging another human being for acceptance and approval. It feels like an insult to your soul, and rightfully so.

To make matters worse, you probably spent a lot of time de-fending yourself to anyone who would listen—waging imaginary arguments and trying to explain your changed position about the relationship, telling others that they weren't actually the perfect partner you once claimed them to be, but instead an abusive psy-chopath.

Unknowingly, survivors often continue to seek approval from external sources long after the relationship has ended. It's a habit that you picked up after placing all of your self-worth in the psychopath's oscillating opinions. When you continue these patterns with others, you might end up with some embarrassing memories—especially if you had always prided yourself on being independent and positive.

It's sort of like a big dark cloud over your otherwise good track record. Your life became a bag of marbles, spilling all over the floor. Your thoughts and emotions scattered everywhere, making it impossible to find clarity and truth. Then slowly, over the course of many months, you began putting the marbles back into the bag. The longer you did this, the more you started to understand what really happened and how your behavior might have come across to others.

But don't worry about this anymore. Forgive yourself and move on—everyone else has. Nobody thinks about you as much as you do. That might sound rude, but I think it's more humbling than anything else. It's a reminder that everyone fights their own battles every single day, and most people won't even remember the embarrassing thing you said a week ago unless you continually bring it up.

Your goal is to focus on the present. There are so many good things coming your way. You will discover more about yourself and this world than you could ever imagine. Because the thing about missing marbles is that you have to search in strange places to find them.

Cognitive Dissonance Returns

The old saying goes that time heals all wounds, and that's true to an extent. The problem with recovery progress is that it encourages you to forget about how bad things really were during the relationship. It's a healing mechanism for your heart—selective amnesia to protect you from the painful memories. You might find yourself thinking about forgiveness and meeting up with your ex for lunch, just to find some peace from the whole thing.

Don't make this mistake: you will just be dragged right back into the same old mind games. You are only projecting your recovered state of happiness and optimism onto your memory of the relationship. This is actually healthy, because it helps to quell the racing thoughts. But you absolutely should not act on these improving moods. Take note of the progress and attribute it to your own efforts. Understand that you are feeling better *because* of your time spent away from the psychopath—not because you're ready to seek closure. Bringing them into your life again will only throw you back to the earlier stages.

I will go into much greater detail about forgiving your abuser in the final chapter of this book. For now, your only job is to continue No Contact and treat yourself kindly.

Trauma and the Two Worlds

One of the most bizarre parts of recovery is feeling as if there are two "yous": The cheerful, trusting soul from before the abuse. And the abrasive, paranoid mess that you fear you've now become. But I think there's something else going on here.

Instead of two yous, let's say there are two worlds. The material world that you see and hear every day. And then another one that you can feel only in your heart—a special connection with the universe and all beings. As kids, I think we're born with a natural link to both. But as we become socialized and grow up, we develop a stronger preference for the first. Slowly, our connection with the quiet world weakens.

To make up for this, we begin to develop a powerful guard—something to keep us safe and confident in the world we've chosen. This guard takes care of our deepest insecurities, vanities, and failures. We learn to judge outwardly, instead of perceiving inwardly. Things are comfortable. From day one, we are developing this guard, teaching us how to be "strong." Strong, of course, being completely defined by the material world.

And then, throughout the course of life, adversity wears away at our guard like sandpaper—hardship, loss, and heartbreak. Slowly, we rebuild this connection with the other world, gaining wisdom and a gentle compassion for the people around us. We look back at our younger selves in embarrassment, wondering how we could have been so obnoxious. At least, that's how I imagine it goes.

But trauma is different.

Instead of sandpaper, the guard is shattered in a single moment. Whatever the damage, your guard is not nearly enough to save you from something so painful. So it collapses, and it can never be rebuilt.

During this brutal disconnect, you lash out and cause harm to others. You overfocus on their behavior, unable to recognize your own—after all, this is what you've become accustomed to. You're dependent and needy, desperately latching on to anyone who will hear your story. You become numb to the things that once made you happy, fondly recalling an "old self" who seemed so much more cheerful.

You are indeed a mess. But in which world?

As you heal from your wounds, you begin to find peace in places you haven't explored since childhood. Imagination. Spirituality. Love. And I mean real love—not the narcissistic, hypervalidating garbage that we craved from a psychopath. You start to fill your void with empathy and compassion, qualities that have been with you since the very beginning.

Mindless socializing doesn't do it for you anymore. You seek out deep, philosophical conversations with like-minded individuals. You often find that you don't fit into various social settings that you used to enjoy. You become frustrated when people don't understand why topics like psychopathy and empathy are so important. You forget that most people still live comfortably with their worldly guard—as you once did—and therefore remain unaffected by these issues.

You struggle to navigate between these two worlds, blaming your difficulty on the two yous. You find that no matter how hard you try, you can never go back to that old self—the person who seemed so much happier and more innocent. But you also start to notice that your interactions with others are becoming much healthier. You've developed boundaries, self-respect, and self-worth. You do not need your worldly guard to be yourself, and that is a strange realization indeed.

And with time, you find that you don't need a guard to be happy at all. For once, self-respect actually comes from—well—the self. You see how much this universe has to offer to those who listen.

As you become more comfortable with yourself, you see that your trauma did not destroy you. It ripped apart your guard and opened a connection with some other world—with all of humanity. You have not lost your childlike wonder. It has been with you all along, and now you are wise enough to live peacefully in both worlds. With joy and wisdom.

You can feel the pain of others, and therefore create much deeper and more meaningful relationships. You understand that what you have is special, and cannot be shared with just anyone. You find peace from listening to the quiet corners of the world. You do not mind time alone, for that is simply time in another world.

The most important thing to remember for all trauma survivors: there is nothing wrong with you. You are beautiful. You were thrown into an impossible situation, and you survived. Your innocence was taken away without your permission. You were violated. But in this violation, you regained something that takes most people a lifetime to find.

Your path may be painful, but it is also special. The universe has different plans for you. Remember, there are others who are permanently barred from any access to the spiritual world. Psychopaths have no place there, and it is why they hate empathetic beings. You are a nagging reminder of something they will never find. They will die here in the material world, with no deeper connection to this great universe.

Sometimes, I believe the spirit world leaks into this one. You can feel it. An overwhelming sadness, when it is not your sadness. Joy for a friend, when it is not your joy. A strange "coincidence" when two people are thinking of each other. Even through this book, I believe we are all connected.

So now imagine these two worlds merging. A place where feelings and compassion are apparent, manifesting themselves for all to see. Where our spirits soar together like birds, singing songs of joy. We can see each other's pain—thorny vines wrapped around a troubled soul. The flickering lights in a victim's spirit. But we also see each other's joy—bright colors and glowing lights emanating from our hearts.

This would be an incredible world for us, but not for the psychopaths. Because if the worlds merged, it would be a world of empathy where psychopaths cannot exist.

So let us work together to bring these two worlds closer. To dismiss darkness, and to teach all empathetic human beings that they are beautiful. Never be ashamed of your abuse or your past. You are here now for a reason—and this is only the beginning.

The Loss of Innocence

Symptoms: profound sadness, mourning, loneliness, acceptance, seeing the world in a different way, hope, accidental wisdom.

There is a difference between sadness and depression. Depression is hopeless, frightening, and mind-numbing. But sadness is beautiful—the gentle moment when your spirit prepares itself for a fresh start.

When you begin to feel real sadness, it's a sign that you're reaching the light at the end of the tunnel. Instead of devastating emptiness and upsetting triggers, your heart is ready to make one last transition. You're done mourning the loss of your soul mate—and instead, you are finally ready to mourn for yourself. You go from a perpetual state of thinking about someone else to suddenly thinking about what *you* lost during all of this.

And most survivors find that they've lost a lot: friendships, money, career opportunities, self-esteem, health, and dignity. Fortunately, these losses can all be reversed. You find that as you return to your roots, all of these things fall back into place. Some will even improve—especially friendships and relationships.

But there's one thing you will never be able to get back: your innocence. Keep in mind that innocence has nothing to do with ignorance or naïveté. It's simply the well-intentioned belief that all human beings have some good in them—the trust and love that you wholeheartedly gave to someone else. That's innocence.

Moving forward, you will never see the world like that again.

That's not to say you're now hypervigilant and jaded. It just means that you're going to view the world and the people around you in a more realistic light. Instead of automatically projecting your own goodness onto others, you let their actions speak for themselves. You see, this is not at all a bad thing. It's just sad at first, because you can never know you're losing your innocence until it's actually gone.

Many survivors find that they didn't really know how to express sadness or anger throughout most of their lives. They were instead expected to be a cheerful servant to everyone around them. And so they developed this stubborn light in their hearts that always sought to see the best in everything, no matter how much the evidence pointed to the contrary.

But you will come to see that the psychopath is something that your heart can never light up. And you will try. That's what cognitive dissonance is all about. For months, you oscillated between the idealization and devaluing phases, trying to understand which one was real. You reasoned that of course they loved you, because they said they did. But then you looked at their actions, which did not at all reflect their words. You know intuitively that love is not insulting, criticizing, cheating, and lying. Love does not make you feel suicidal. Love does not mock you for having hurt feelings.

And so, the more you thought about it, the angrier and more depressed you got. The light inside of you began to fade away as this person consumed your every thought. The light could not transform their behavior, so instead it started to absorb it, growing dimmer every day.

As time went on, you felt profound rage and an emptiness that you'd never felt in your life. Throughout most of the process, you probably didn't even know how to express it. So on the outside, you remained this happy person that everyone expected and needed. You wouldn't want to inconvenience anyone with your feelings. But deep down, something was changing. The light was almost out, and suddenly you found yourself feeling very resentful and irritated with many people—people you thought were your friends.

After each interaction, you'd return home and find yourself reflecting for hours on what had just taken place. Who was that? It wasn't you. You didn't truly believe the things you were saying, and you certainly held no respect for the gossip and insults they so adored. Suddenly your light isn't justifying it all away as humor anymore. You're just left with the cold reality that you've surrounded yourself with some very unkind people.

You're left as a drained battery that's still expected to fuel a rocket. Your energy is broken. You want to automatically love everyone like you used to, but you can't. Unkindness and superficiality frustrate you when they never did before.

For a long time, you probably remembered the psychopath so fondly not because they were a good person, but because of your own light. You were rewarded every single day for denying the bad and glorifying the mediocre. You now associate that relationship with your light, but that does not mean they actually made you happy. It means your innocence made you happy, because it was protecting your very gentle heart.

The ability to distinguish your innocence from genuine happiness is essential to your healing process. Simply because you once felt euphoric with the psychopath and with friends who frequently insulted you does not mean that life was actually great at the time. Likewise, just because you feel sadness now does not mean that your life is somehow bad. On the contrary, things are looking brighter than ever before. You're just struggling to enjoy the world without your light.

But you don't have to. Your light never left you—it's just waiting. Yes, it's a bit shy right now. But as you begin to develop your self-respect and boundaries, the light will flicker back on. And as you explore your love and spirituality, the light will return stronger than ever.

So many survivors long to go back to a time when life was "normal" and "happy," but how much of that was ever real? How much of that time did you spend desperately trying to replace the negative with positive? How much of it was projection, while other people were busy projecting their own poison onto you? When your light fades, especially after a trauma like this, it becomes far more difficult to keep projecting goodness onto others.

So I believe that you do not truly miss your past, but instead you miss the light you associate with it.

One thing I've noticed about every member on Psychopath Free.com is that none of them want to feel this darkness. Not a single one. They do not want to be victims. They want to recover their happiness and joy. They feel a burning anger about being angry in the first place. They've practiced forgiveness throughout their entire lives, only to be confronted with the most unforgivable experience of a psychopath. Why? What was the point? Why did their identity need to be destroyed like this, leaving them so incredibly broken and drained?

With time, you will find your own answers to these questions. Your innocence was a beautiful gift, but the paradox was that you never knew you had it. This was why you tended to pour so much of your love and affection into other human beings. Because you hadn't yet felt that love for yourself. Through the healing process, you make that final leap. As uncomfortable as it may be, you find self-respect and begin creating healthy boundaries. Instead of trying to fit in with others, you find yourself wondering why people don't behave more like you. Empathetic, compassionate, loving, outgoing, creative, easygoing, responsible, caring . . . The gentle souls who walk this earth and touch it only with kindness.

When your light is gone, you can no longer use it to fix all of the broken things around you. So in its place, you begin to surround yourself with people who actually share and appreciate your most wonderful qualities. And you can't discover all of that magic until your innocence is gone, giving you an opportunity to see the world as it truly is—as you truly are.

This journey is about you, and it always has been. Once you discover this, you are finally ready to fly free.

freedom

You can free your spirit with the very same imagination you once used to imprison it. With this knowledge, you take full responsibility for the person you're about to become.

Looking Back, Moving Forward

Once you have truly and completely disconnected your spirit from the psychopath, you will be able to look back on the experience from a less emotional perspective. You will begin to understand that you are not missing out on anything—in fact, you got lucky.

I know it doesn't seem like that at first. It always feels like they're winning, because that's the image they present to the world. Psychopaths always seem to be winning because they manage to abuse and replace victims with a big smile on their face, all the while appearing innocent and cheerful to the entire world. While you're at rock bottom, they seem to be happier than ever with their new life. But it's all an illusion—manufactured success to impress others and evoke negative feelings in their past victims. This is not the behavior of a winner. This is the behavior of a loser desperately trying to convince themselves and others that they are superior. A psychopath is incapable of feeling all of the most wonderful human emotions: love, trust, and compassion. Sure, they pulled off their latest con with great success, but just because a person gets what they want does not make them a winner.

So they pranced off into the sunset with some other partner, but you've forgotten about something very important. How can any single human being go from being so abusive to a sudden, new, and perfect relationship with someone else? They can't. It's emotionally and logically impossible.

You might wish they would break up with the new victim, just for the validation. But it won't make any difference. The psychopath will repeat their cycle until the day they die or settle down with a comfortable target. You do not need to stick around and watch. They'll maintain the shallow illusion of success and happiness no matter what happens. You will never gain any satisfaction from their downfall. Instead, you will come to understand that their entire life is a failure—a sham.

The Anomaly

a·nom·a·ly (noun): something that deviates from what is standard, normal, or expected.

During and after an encounter with a psychopath, you probably found yourself behaving in ways you never imagined: lashing out, pleading, begging, taking revenge, writing nasty letters, apologizing profusely, blaming yourself, blaming others—a far cry from your usual fun-loving, easygoing self. You probably feel ashamed about this behavior, but it's time to let that go. Any emotionally healthy human being is going to react strongly to emotional abuse. The fact that you're ashamed about it means you have a conscience.

During the idealization, you were tricked into a frenzied excitement. During the abuse, you were doing everything you could to hang on to that manufactured dream. During the silence, you were frantically trying to figure out what you did wrong (did you know that silence sets off the same receptors in the brain as physical pain?). And after that, you saw your abuser happily run off with another person as if you never existed.

How is anyone's heart supposed to withstand all of that?

The answer is: it can't. That's why your entire personality seemed to transform into someone you barely recognized. Your emotional responses imploded upon one another, all in a very human attempt to respond to a completely inhuman experience. And now you're left with a lot of embarrassing memories and concerns about your own good nature.

But was any of this behavior normal for you?

I'm a visual person, so I made this chart to illustrate what I'm trying to say:

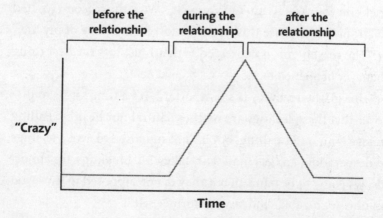

Before this person entered your life, you never behaved like this. After this person was gone from your life, you never behaved like this. So what does that tell you?

Assuming an average human baseline level of partly crazy, along with some expected craziness during the recovery period, the spike in the chart still seems abnormally huge (scientifically speaking, of course). If you take into account that this spike never existed in any of your other relationships, suddenly we have some very compelling evidence that suggests this "craziness" might actually be an anomaly.

This anomaly was situational—specific only to this very strange and very hurtful experience. During the recovery stages, it takes quite some time for things to settle back down into a healthy (likely healthier) equilibrium, but the point is: the process only begins once you've gone No Contact with this person, and not a moment sooner. So what does this really say about their influence on you? Was it positive or negative? Looking back at your Constant, did you ever experience these strange spikes with them?

Now keep in mind, your brain is probably going to play some tricks on you. You'll think to yourself, "Well, the reason I reacted so strongly is because this was the most intense love of my life," or "The reason I'm so depressed is that I just lost the best thing that ever happened to me."

This is why recovery is so important. It's a time for us to discover that these feelings are neither natural nor healthy. Falling in love is an intense thing, but it's not supposed to evoke feelings of desperation, anxiety, and fear. Likewise, breakups are almost always going to be painful, but they're not supposed to leave you an unrecognizable shell of your former self.

Psychopaths would love for you to believe that this was a perfectly healthy relationship—that you just fell too hard and too fast. In fact, they scoff at the idea that anyone should need to "recover" from them, because they do not feel things like heartbreak and devastation. So the next time your friends, family, or ex-partner make you feel guilty for the time it's taking you to heal, remember that your recovery path is also an anomaly. You're allowed to take as much time and energy as you need to feel better, because you're recovering from an experience that hugely deviated from the norm.

So wherever you are now—whether it be in the midst of an abusive relationship, emptiness after the breakup, or shame for your own uncharacteristic behavior—forgive yourself. If you've spent your whole life being patient and kind with others, don't start questioning your entire sense of self now, just because of what this relationship did to you. Look back at those moments, accept that it was unusual, and be gentle with yourself.

You've taken responsibility for your anomaly. A psychopath will never take responsibility for the way they behave *every single day*.

A Letter to the Next Target

In nearly every toxic relationship, there is another player: the replacement. At first, this person is the main source of contention and hatred in your recovery journey. They are presumed to be the home wrecker. They ran off happily with your soul mate, flaunting themselves all over Facebook, while you became the crazy, jealous ex. This person stole your dream.

But with time, you come to see that this person actually saved your life.

This is a letter for every "next target." I'm not suggesting you send it to anyone. That wouldn't accomplish a thing and would only serve to hurt you, pull you back in. But we all want to get to the point where we can write this letter, and I suspect we would all wish, in retrospect, that it was a letter we were sent.

Dear _____:

I cannot reach you directly, for it would only send me back into a world of insanity that I have no desire to revisit. But I can hope that you might come across this letter and learn that there are always two sides to every story. You have already been told one. Here is the other.

I hated you. I watched you run off with the love of my life, happily and shamelessly showing the world what you had done. It took me weeks to realize that the infidelity had been going on long before our relationship ended. It took me months to realize that my pain and tears were used as a device to manufacture your sympathy. And now it will take me years to recover from the insecurity that comes from being triangulated with another person.

But I do not hate you anymore. I fear for you.

Although we have different personalities, bodies, and spirits—when it comes to this relationship, we are no different.

You see, I once rode the high that you're currently riding. I was the special one. The most beautiful, perfect, flawless part-

ner in the world. I saved them from the pain inflicted by their last, crazy ex. I sympathized with them about how horribly they were treated. I was elated to be the one who finally made them happy after all of their alleged suffering. They were fascinated by me. They spent every waking moment texting me and showering me with attention.

Does this sound familiar?

One must wonder, in this short span of time, how I suddenly became crazy. Bipolar. Jealous. Needy. Clingy. Abusive. How did that happen? Is it really possible for a person to go from flawless to horrible in the blink of an eye? And furthermore, is it really possible that their previous ex was all of these things as well? And what about the ex before that?

The common denominator has become startlingly clear.

For so long, I punished myself. I truly believed that I deserved my pain. Something must be wrong with me, I thought, in order for them to run off into the sunset with another person.

But then I realized, I was once that person. I was you.

And because of that, I understand that I can never save you from this nightmare. Victims of psychopaths cannot escape once they have been groomed. For the rest of your relationship, you will deny reality and invent reasons that you might be the exception. You will lie to yourself, desperately trying to re-create your perfect dream. But ever so slowly, your identity will begin to fall apart. They will push your boundaries until you don't even know who you are anymore.

Another person will enter the scene. It is inevitable in relationships with narcissistic predators. You will be strung along for as long as possible, as I once was. Your increasingly volatile reactions will be used against you, to evoke sympathy from the new target.

And eventually, you will be me.

This is why I fear for you. I would not wish the pain and suffering I've experienced on anyone. I know that your intentions were not malicious. I know that you were being spoon-fed the exact same lies I believed a long time ago.

The story you've been told is false. It was a pity ploy, designed to enhance your fairy tale and consume your heart. You will not believe that today, but someday this letter will make sense. Brutal, heartbreaking sense.

I can only hope that the aftermath of your abuse might be guided by this letter. I can only hope that this might provide you with the tools that I was never given. A puzzle piece, to jump-start your journey.

I do not hate you. That is what they would want.

I will not carry on their legacy by taking part in these triangles anymore, injecting jealousy and hatred to fill the void of their soul.

I've made it through to the other side, and I know you can, too. Please have the same empathy for the person who replaces you. We can only ever stop this cycle of abuse with compassion for one another, by recognizing that all human beings deserve to be treated with respect, kindness, and honesty.

Wishing you love, hope, and above all: freedom.

Introspection and Insecurities

You were manipulated, insulted, degraded, belittled, and neglected. Full responsibility for this goes to the psychopath. It does not matter if you were vulnerable or insecure—no decent human being should ever take advantage of another. None of it was your fault.

By now, you may have educated yourself about psychopathic behavior, learned the signs, and validated your experience. You should be disgusted by the psychopath's behavior and have no desire to see them ever again. I hope you have found a comfortable landing place after experiencing the stages of grief—on the road to self-forgiveness, healing, and love. But you may still be stuck in a place of insecurity, not trusting your judgment, thinking that you were blind enough to fall for a psychopath and worried that you cannot trust yourself to make good decisions going forward. Hopefully you've reached out to a healing professional or a recovery group, and have found the support you need to recover from the trauma you have suffered, and you will find sure footing as you walk into a psychopath-free life.

However, as essential as support is, there comes a time when you need to start trusting yourself again. This book and the Psychopath Free forum are not crutches—they are stepping-stones. Sooner or later, all survivors must learn to make decisions on their own, without seeking the opinions of everyone around them. Better life choices can only come from within, and you will know when you're making them because your intuition and self-respect will skyrocket. You certainly won't need to seek any external approval.

Introspection is a great way to discover why you're looking for this approval in the first place. It could be rooted in your childhood, past friendships, the psychopathic relationship—or any combination of the above. In order to better understand how all of this came to be, you can look back on the relationship and examine the toxic dynamic that formed. The psychopath's mirroring techniques are actually an incredible, once-in-a-lifetime opportunity to take a look at your own demons.

Mirror, Mirror on the Wall

It's time to start asking questions. Why did this happen? What are your vulnerabilities? Of course these vulnerabilities aren't your fault, but it is important to understand how you were able to be exploited. This will help you to further deconstruct the bond with your ex, and protect yourself from any future emotional abuse.

This experience is all about cultivating a healthy self-esteem that comes from within, not from any sort of external validation. We all have insecurities and vanities—many of which we're probably not aware of. True self-discovery comes from practicing introspection and becoming aware of those little flaws.

This part is really up to you, but here are some of the most common reasons survivors give for falling for the psychopath in the first place: looks, money, career, an unfulfilling marriage, need for attention, need to be appreciated, fear of being alone. Digging deeper, they find the insecurities that were at the root of their reasons: *Their good looks validated my own attractiveness. I am worried about financial stability and my ability to provide for myself. I was looking for their career success to prove that I'm successful, too. Their attention made me feel beautiful, interesting, worthy, etc.*

Now look at your relationship with the psychopath. Whatever you needed most, they validated and provided. Pay special attention to the specifics of their excessive flattery. These are what you were seeking validation for.

So what are your insecurities? Get out a piece of paper and make a list. This will save your life down the road. Once you're aware of these traits, you will also become aware of the people who try to manipulate them. And even better, you can begin to make changes—to better yourself and improve your life. For example, why should you need someone else to tell you you're attractive in order to feel it in your heart?

Those who have conquered their demons will be completely useless to a psychopath. You won't be susceptible to the psychopath's grooming if you do not require validation, but instead simply enjoy a compliment every now and then. Psychopaths feed on unhealthy needs, not everyday kindness. With time, you will find yourself less and less attracted to those who excessively flatter and praise you.

Keep in mind, there is another kind of vulnerability: the good kind. Your dreams—sexual fantasies, life goals, romantic endeavors, perhaps raising a family—are beautiful, good vulnerabilities that make you human. Do not let the psychopathic experience change these things. Next to your list of insecurities, make a list of your dreams. You must never mistake your passions for flaws. And likewise, your empathetic nature is not a weakness—although the psychopath certainly makes you question that.

Cowardly Love

Psychopaths don't just shower you with praise and flattery— they groom you to reciprocate. In the very beginning, they send constant text messages and want to know what you're doing at every moment. If you don't respond fast enough, they'll send quick follow-ups with more compliments. At first, it seems like they truly need you—like you're the answer to all of their supposed insecurities and crazy exes. You come to rely on this communication as a source of happiness and self-worth. And that's when they start to pull back. Once you're hooked, they'll suddenly start to seem slightly bored and annoyed by your attempts to continue the dynamic that they created. This leads you to feel needy, smothering, and unhinged. Your excitement about finding perfect

> love rapidly transforms into a constant fear of losing it. This is how cowards manufacture "love" in others. Since they are unlovable in their true forms, they learn at an early age how to engineer desperation and desire.

Sympathy for the Devil

Adorable. Charming. Lovable. You'll often hear these adjectives used to describe a psychopath. It's all part of their plan. You were probably never attracted to arrogance, jerkiness, and overconfidence. Instead, you're drawn to the innocent, sympathetic partner— the one who tells you you're making them happier than anyone else. But then something shifts. Instead of being the person that makes them happy, you desperately need them to make you happy. There is a strange pattern among most survivors: going from "giving them attention" to "needing their attention" in the blink of an eye. How did this transition happen? How did you lose your self-esteem to someone who seemed to have none to begin with?

When you first met the psychopath, you probably felt sorry for them. They had so many sympathetic qualities: their ex had abused them, they were insecure about the way they looked, they'd been so unhappy until they met you, etc.

This is where your empathy kicks in. You've done it all your life: you see someone feeling inferior, and you know how to make them feel better. You want to heal them. And so you put all of yourself into raising someone else up.

The psychopath genuinely seems to adore all of your efforts. They compare you to their exes, idealizing you above everyone else. It's as if all of your energies finally have a purpose, and you're so appreciated.

Many survivors report not even being attracted to the psychopath at first. But with time, you begin to see them as the best-looking person in the world. You can't even think of anyone else sexually. How did this happen? By pouring all of your empathetic capital into healing their supposed insecurities, you come to a point where you actually start to believe your own kindness and compassion. You told them how smart, funny, successful, and attractive they were, and you started to believe it yourself.

You also become obsessed with proving your loyalty, because you believe the problem is their insecurity. So you open up to them and tell them how much you need them. If you make yourself vulnerable enough, surely they will learn to overcome their inferiority complex.

But that's not the problem and it never was.

You know now that you spent all this time chasing a manufactured illusion: you were under the impression that they thought they were lucky to be with you. You probably didn't like that power dynamic, so you built up your partner in order to make them feel better. And this is how they hooked you: with sympathy. If you perceive them as childlike, your natural instincts kick in, and you do everything you can to prove how much you care. This is likely the way you've dealt with people throughout your life: when others have no self-confidence, you try to build it for them.

Like a psychopath, you can probably sense insecurities. The difference lies in how you act upon those insecurities. Psychopaths see them as a way to manipulate and control. Empathetic people, on the other hand, seek to cure insecurities with love and compassion. This is why so many survivors find themselves surrounded with negative people after the breakup: because for a long time, they probably gained their sense of self-worth by making miserable people happy.

So when the psychopath came along, you were willing to do whatever it took to build up their happiness. You constantly complimented their looks, you didn't mind paying for dates, you laughed at their jokes even when they weren't funny. And in return, you were rewarded with their overwhelming appreciation that gave your life meaning. Your self-worth was sky-high because they were feeding it.

But somewhere in this whirlwind, you suddenly found the tables turned. It happened fast. Instead of sympathetically reassuring the poor guy or girl, you found yourself desperate for *their* approval. They began to make it clear that they did not actually need all of that attention. In fact, they found it very annoying. When you complimented them, you received an arrogant laugh or a disingenuous "you too baby." It's as if you became the relationship newbie, and they were the one who would take things from there.

Additionally, they made sure you knew that they were getting attention from other sources. Your unique ability to make them happy wasn't so unique after all. This triangulation was pure torture.

They used the silent treatment to punish you and deride your once-needed sympathies. You began to feel stupid, unattractive, needy, and useless. Your solution was to continue sacrificing yourself to make room for their "feelings." You suppressed complaints about their lying or triangulating because they made it very clear that this kind of talk was unacceptable.

Do you see what happened? They made sure the ball was in their court. And the scary thing is, despite your own beliefs, it was never in your court to begin with. All they did was make you believe it was. By giving you this false sense of self-confidence and importance, you opened up fast. This is why you trusted the psychopath very quickly and let them into your life without a second guess.

This is also why the grand finale was more terrible than anything you've ever felt before. It was the outright dismissal of your self-worth. You invested all of it in them, thereby giving them the power to take it away. You never recognized the game they were playing, because you were too busy pleasing their invented childlike persona. After all, how in the world could a child be plotting manipulation and domination? And then they declare "checkmate" when you thought you were playing checkers.

The hard part is that you weren't just addicted to the flattery and attention they gave you. You were actually more addicted to their appreciation of all you gave them, because this appreciation gave you self-worth. Without their appreciation, you feel empty, and that's why the recovery from a psychopathic breakup takes so long. You are not just getting over a romantic encounter; you're rebuilding your self-worth from scratch.

That's also why you become so sensitive to the reactions of future partners. Until you go through the recovery process, you will be bouncing around trying to find a replacement for the approval that you lost—something to give your life meaning again.

But there is good news here, and it outweighs everything else. Once you begin recovery, your life changes forever. You start to find overwhelming self-worth in your own values, behavior, and heart. Remember those negative people I mentioned above? Slowly but surely, they begin to disappear from the picture. At first, you question yourself and remember how "happy" you were with them. But as you redefine your self-worth, you come to realize that *you* created this happiness. And similar to your relationship with the psychopath, you thought these people needed your happiness. Well, this isn't your responsibility anymore. You have better things coming your way.

What's Your Personality?

Do you ever wonder why you hate conflict and criticism, while others seem to have no problem with it? Do you wonder why you enjoy quiet time on your own, while others can't stand it? Do you sometimes feel alone and misunderstood, in that no one else really experiences the world the same way you do?

On the forums, one of our most popular threads is about the Myers-Briggs personality test. If you haven't ever taken it, you definitely should! Visit Personalities.PsychopathFree.com to check out the quick quiz, read about each personality type, and see other survivors' results. Essentially, it's a type indicator that looks at how you make decisions and perceive the world. Then it places you into one of sixteen different personality types.

Of course, every human being is unique and won't fit perfectly into a box with billions of other people, but many survivors have found the test to be hugely helpful in understanding their own personalities. Each personality type is composed of four letters, with each letter belonging to a category having two possibilities:

1. I (Introvert) / E (Extrovert)
2. S (Sensing) / N (iNtuitive)
3. T (Thinking) / F (Feeling)
4. P (Perceiving) / J (Judging)

My type is INFP—the Idealists—and when I discovered this test, I realized a lot of important things about myself.

First of all, introverts are allowed to be introverts. I spent most of my life trying to surround myself with as many friends as possible to prove that I was having fun, but secretly I usually wanted to be alone out by the river, watching the sunset and thinking about stuff. Well, now it's not a secret! I am free to enjoy time by myself without feeling that there's something wrong with me.

The next part (iNtuitive over Sensing) just means I'm more big-picture-oriented. In case you can't tell from my "research" throughout this book, I don't really care about details very much. I am much more interested in the world as a whole—how humans interact with one another on a broader scale, and how we can describe these feelings in a way that others can understand.

The F part (Feeling over Thinking) wasn't exactly a big surprise. I walk around the city randomly crying to sad classical music, which is probably really weird to the other pedestrians.

The last one (Perceiving over Judging) means I tend not to like deadlines, structure, or having my weekends filled up with plans. It also means I would be well suited to be with someone who remembers to do things like pay bills or turn off the stove that time I got distracted by cat pictures and almost burned down my apartment.

So put all of that together, and what do you get? A complete basket case! Wait, no, I mean—an Idealist! Yes, that sounds much better.

As I learned more about my type, I also discovered some important challenges. First of all, INFPs have pretty intense mood swings every once in a while, where suddenly all of our bad memories come creeping back and make it feel like we're never going to be happy again. I rarely share these moods with others and instead seek out alone time to work through the feelings on my own. After a sunny walk or a solid night of sleep, I find that these moods go away and life is good again. Learning to cope with these dark spells has been a key part of my own recovery and growth. I'm still working on it!

Here's another one: INFPs are usually extremely easygoing, unless one of our principal values has been violated. Then we defend those things in an uncharacteristically rigid way. So instead of sometimes turning into a gigantic butthead, I have found that I am most content spending my time with people who do not violate my values to begin with. Then I never become harsh or rigid in a way that I know I'll later regret.

I'm poking fun at myself, but that's kind of the point. When we learn about ourselves, we can become more balanced and take our flaws a bit more lightly, instead of blindly allowing them to dictate our lives. This makes it far easier to enjoy our strengths.

Let's do one more: INFPs place a great deal of importance in our romantic relationships, feeling an unusual amount of love and loyalty for our partners. Sometimes this means romanticizing qualities in others that don't actually exist, mainly because we want to be able to love everything about them. When I realized that it's okay to love myself regardless of my own flaws, I also became much more comfortable loving others regardless of their flaws.

If personality analysis sounds fun to you, I really recommend taking the test! Maybe it won't mean much, but I think you'll discover some pretty cool stuff about yourself.

Alone Time

Full disclosure: I am actually relieved when people cancel plans on me, so I may be a bit of an outlier on this topic. But even so, I think quiet time alone can really be beneficial. We live in such a fast-paced, constantly changing world where there are temporary distractions and stimuli at every turn. Instead of spending a night reflecting on the day, we turn to TV or the Internet to dull the boredom and relax. This makes sense after a tiring day, but we also miss out on a lot of opportunities for self-improvement.

There's so much you can do on your own: meditation, journaling, painting, gardening, cooking, walking, working out, listening to music—the list could go on forever. When we get more comfortable spending time on our own, we learn a lot about ourselves. At first, it can all be a little bit daunting—especially if we have negative things on our mind. It's not very fun to spend time with those thoughts.

But that's the magic of alone time! You are completely and 100 percent in control of your own happiness. You can imagine anything you want, transforming a bad mood into a good one. Or maybe you want to feel the bad mood fully, in which case you can cry all you want, and nobody can judge you. When you're alone, there's no pressure to be someone you're not. For a while I actually used to need time alone in order to remember who I was. When we're constantly surrounded by people—especially toxic influences—it becomes really easy to forget ourselves. We get caught up in drama, gossip, and negativity.

This is especially true after the psychopathic encounter. The psychopath becomes our entire life, and we find ourselves consumed by daily arguments, lies, gaslighting, and manipulation. Instead of being our true selves, we transform into an extension of them, constantly trying to understand and defend ourselves from their mind-boggling behavior.

So what happens when all of that is finally gone from our lives? It seems like everything should be blissful, but most of us know that's not the case. It's difficult to just slow down and relax after we've become accustomed to such a high level of drama. What's going to fill that void?

This is why alone time is so important.

Our mind has been on overdrive for so long, it needs some dedicated discipline to take a step back and remember what it's like to live a life *without* all that drama. Without constantly trying to gain someone else's approval. Without fearing that you've made one small misstep that could ruin everything. Without playing detective because someone else's behavior is sketchy. Without the love-bombing and flattery that once made you feel so good.

When we're alone, we don't have any of those external factors swaying our behavior. There is nobody to validate (or invalidate) our thoughts except ourselves. We're our most authentic and raw selves, which can be scary or enlightening, depending on your perspective.

For me, it was a little bit of both. Scary at first, because I really didn't like myself at all when I finally started to take a step back and look at my life. I'd done a lot of awful things after our breakup, and I had deluded myself into thinking that it was all for some noble cause to warn or help others. In reality, it was nothing more than obsessive revenge. After a while, I realized that it wasn't my ex's behavior that upset me any longer—he rarely crossed my mind anymore. It was my own subsequent behavior that I still struggled to understand and accept. How did I become that monster? How could I learn to forgive myself for such deplorable behavior? I violated my own code of ethics and values, which I believe to be the very foundation of a person's character. I encountered my own darkness, and it was ugly. There was no taking those things back. There was no blaming someone else for my own actions.

Right after the breakup it was like I had entered some sort of manic train-wreck state that couldn't be stopped. But, like most undesirable emotions, it's just a matter of teaching the brain new habits. At first, it was frustrating. I'd have a nice quiet week where I finally stopped dating and trying to replace the "love" I lost. The next weekend, I'd suddenly get the urge to go out and I'd end up right back in that same manic state. Everything would come crashing down from one stupid decision.

But it's always two steps forward, one step back.

Eventually, I found that I actually preferred the quiet time by myself. The thought of going out was exhausting. The thought of spending time with negative people was exhausting. I stopped giving in to other people—even well-intentioned ones—and just didn't do things that I didn't want to do. Something in my brain really was rewiring. I started going outside a lot and thinking about stuff and myself. I'd always dreamed of writing books, so I actually wrote books! I was in touch with a completely different set of emotions, and that old scary train wreck wasn't anywhere to be found.

Over the summer, I started this new hobby of swimming in the river and watching the sunset with some sweet white wine over ice. Instead of triggering "OMG I NEED A BOYFRIEND" mode, it just makes me happy. To this day, I sit there for hours after work and imagine story ideas, completely in awe of the beautiful world and people around me.

When you are the most important person who can disappoint or inspire you, everything becomes very exciting. It also becomes quieter. Because it's a lot easier to be a quiet, genuine version of you than it is to frantically maintain a loud version of you that isn't really you at all. If you find yourself desperately trying to prove to the rest of the world that a certain version of yourself is the real you, then it's probably not the truest version of you.

I used to be afraid of spending time alone, afraid of facing ugly truths about myself and my life. But now I'm mostly at peace with myself. Sure, I'm still scatterbrained, insecure, and moody—but those things don't control my life anymore. They're just little puzzles that I work on when I'm diving into the water.

Self-Respect

Psychopaths create chaos wherever they go, all the while maintaining a cover of complete innocence. They steamroll straight through each target's life, leaving behind nothing but destruction and confusion. Responsible, successful people suddenly find everything falling apart—from once-stable, cheerful friendships to careers to self-esteem. In a matter of months, even weeks, a psychopath will effectively destroy all of the harmony and trust you've spent your entire life building. They walk into your life, charm you into trusting them, engineer paranoia and panic, and then watch intently as you fall from grace. In the end, they disappear without another word, leaving you alone to pick up the pieces. You end up questioning your sanity—your very understanding of reality. But with time, you come to fill this darkness with qualities you perhaps never valued in yourself: empathy, compassion, kindness, and creativity. In their efforts to destroy and deceive, psychopaths always underestimate a dreamer's strength. We may not be ruthless, but we are resilient.

At some point, you will find that instead of trying to gain everyone else's approval, you are wondering why people can't be more like you. Why can't they be easygoing, kind, caring, selfless, accommodating, and self-aware? This is called self-respect. This is your self-worth coming from within. Of course it still feels good to make someone else happy, but now you have a much better measure of who deserves your light. And this will bring you joy for the rest of your life.

You will also begin to discover that the psychopath targeted you specifically because of these assets. This does not make them weaknesses; all you needed was the self-awareness and self-respect to take pride in them. To quote my honorary aunt Peru: "[Psychopaths] are fascinated with human emotion and are forever honing their craft of mimicking 'normal.' Empathetic people have the full spectrum of emotions, so it's like a master class for them. Also, [psychopaths] can suck out of these people the life force they lack. Giving and trusting, empathetic people make perfect targets." And of course, there is nothing wrong with being giving and trusting. Self-respect is simply about coming to expect the same thing from others.

This is when you begin to discover all of your strengths. Many of these were qualities you always possessed but never valued. You realize that your compassion, empathy, and love are not weaknesses; they are the most incredible gifts in the world, when applied to the right people. You start to understand who you're truly meant to be. It took the psychopath's cruelty to make you see exactly who you never want to be. You laugh at their earlier mirroring, when they told you that the two of you are so much alike, because you realize you are nothing like them. You begin to explore your creative side, and you stop caring what others think of you. Old friendships may also start to change as you change and become more confident. Your boundaries are returning, or perhaps being formed for the very first time.

Boundaries

Building boundaries is one of the most difficult parts about developing self-respect. It feels unnatural, almost psychopathic at first. How can you be strict with people who need your help? And moreover, how do you deal with those who accuse you of being unreasonable or hypersensitive because you're no longer their doormat?

You must come to differentiate unreasonableness and hypersensitivity from healthy boundaries. The people who accuse you of being unreasonable are very likely to be abrasive, rude, or unpleasant themselves. The only difference is, now you're not their doormat. They will do whatever they can to maintain the existing dynamic, because more boundaries mean less complacency. You should never feel the need to defend yourself against a friend. You should never have to explain why you can't make plans one evening. And you should never be walking on eggshells, trying to rephrase a text to avoid an unpleasant interaction.

These people-pleasing habits are toxic to you, and often stem from a need to make others happy. But sometimes, there isn't any deeper origin to these patterns beyond simply being a gentle person. If you naturally tend to be agreeable and friendly, toxic people will sense this and latch on to you. They quickly discover how to manipulate you with guilt-tripping, passive aggression, and martyrdom. This snowballs, as more and more of these people find you. You become stuck in their cycles of insecurity, which is often the reason you're already desensitized to the psychopath's abuse.

When Not to Say "I'm Sorry"

Gentle people tend to feel very guilty after they stand up for themselves or reprimand someone for inappropriate behavior. This immediate apology for maintaining boundaries is exploited by toxic people. They come to expect your self-inflicted anguish, and know that they don't actually need to change their behavior, because you'll feel bad soon enough anyway. Additionally, your desire to reconcile allows them to call you "bipolar," for alternating so quickly between firmness and compassion.

You should always feel comfortable sitting down with a friend and mentioning a concern. Normal people are receptive to suggestions for improving themselves, especially if they're phrased kindly. Empathetic people should be especially invested in making sure they haven't hurt your feelings. But toxic people will instead blow up, turning the conversation back on you. Or they'll blame their past and offer up fake apologies, only to continue the exact same behavior the following week. If you find yourself repeatedly excusing someone else's bad behavior, stop and consider why they couldn't simply behave in a way that didn't require excusing to begin with.

Channeling Empathy

A lot of people live by a simple motto: always be kind. They believe that as long as they're nice, the world will be nice back. But as many of us have discovered, this isn't the way things work. There are people out there who seek to exploit kindness, which ultimately results in our spirits being reduced to rubble. And so once we recover from these experiences, our first reaction is to declare war against our previous selves. No more compassion, flexibility, and generosity—screw it all! But that is not a very good solution. The problem was never your kindness; the problem was those who manipulated it. Love and empathy are what make a dreamer's life so fulfilling. It's what gives us this unique connection with the world and people around us. Don't throw that away because you've been hurt. Instead, throw away the people who hurt you to begin with. Save your gifts for those who can truly appreciate and reciprocate them. Your Constant is probably an example of one of these people. Abusers, on the other hand, manipulate your greatest qualities and make you doubt yourself.

So how can you live healthily in a world where you are bound to encounter both good and bad people every day? How can you stand up for yourself and still retain a strong sense of your gentle, compassionate nature? The answer lies in learning to "channel" your empathy—to disconnect from toxic people, and not feel bad for doing so.

The loss of innocence is your heart's way of beginning this path. Now that you're learning to discover who's healthy and who's not, you understand that you are not obligated to make everyone around you happy. You can find the greatest peace by surrounding yourself with a small, trusted group of warmhearted people. Then you will be free to exercise all of your compassion, without feeling exhausted and drained.

Around toxic people, however, you will start to put these abilities on hold. This doesn't mean you somehow become a temporary psychopath (is there even such a thing?). All you're doing is protecting your spirit. This means perceiving with your brain instead of your heart. Your heart will always be ready to trust and believe the best in others. But your brain will provide you with a logical, objective assessment of the situation. This is the best way to deal with toxic people. You do not need to waste your emotional capital on them. You only have so much, and you deserve to spend it on the people who make you happy.

The healing process is all about learning to discover your true strengths, and surrounding yourself with people who share and appreciate those qualities. From there, everything starts to change. The dreamer's journey is universal and strangely circular—returning to the wisdom we've always had but never recognized.

The Psychopath-Free Pledge

When members first join our forum we ask them to take a pledge. It's a promise that honors self-respect and encourages healthy relationships. If you follow these simple affirmations, you will find permanent freedom from toxic bonds:

1. I will never beg or plead for someone else again. Any man or woman who brings me to that level is not worth my heart.

2. I will never tolerate criticisms about my body, age, weight, job, or any other insecurities I might have. Good partners won't put me down; they'll raise me up.

3. I will take a step back to objectively look at my relationship at least once every month to make sure that I am being respected and loved, not flattered and love-bombed.

4. I will always ask myself the question "Would I ever treat someone else like this?" If the answer is no, then I don't deserve to be treated like that either.

5. I will trust my gut. If I get a bad feeling, I won't try to push it away and make excuses. I will trust myself.

6. I understand that it is better to be single than in a toxic relationship.

7. I will not be spoken to in a condescending or sarcastic way. Loving partners will not patronize me.

8. I will not allow my partner to call me jealous, crazy, or any other dismissive accusations.

9. My relationships will be mutual and equal at all times. Love is not about control and power.

10. If I ever feel unsure about any of these steps, I will seek out help from a friend, support forum, or therapist. I will not act on impulsive decisions.

Do you take the pledge? If so, sign your name on this page as a reminder—so you can come back anytime and remember the promise you made to yourself. Treating yourself kindly not only accelerates the healing process, it also sets healthier habits in motion that will carry on throughout your future relationships and friendships. So do yourself a favor, and train your mind to start expecting the good things you've always deserved.

Authenticity

The recovery process is the beginning of your new life. You'll look back at old dynamics, wondering how you ever tolerated such toxicity. As I mentioned earlier, you might even feel embarrassed about your past behavior. This regret is your self-respect kicking in, reminding you that you're different now.

After the relationship, you probably felt yourself "cheerleading" a lot, handing out compliments as a way to receive them back yourself. You may especially do this with other abuse victims. With time, your compliments will start to become much more personal and sincere. You develop strong friendships with people whom you truly care about, instead of just selflessly throwing yourself at every survivor you meet along the way. This is healthy. The world is a big place. You shouldn't be best friends with everyone you come across. It's far better to have a few good friends than a million acquaintances with whom you exchange shallow formalities.

Along those same lines, survivors who spend their days helping other abuse victims should be proud of themselves. Whether it be online, in person, or over the phone, you're doing something incredible to change the world. Abuse recovery is a part of who you are, and you should feel comfortable sharing this with friends and partners. You work with survivors, and that's a passion worth cultivating.

For a long time, I felt weird telling people about this book and the Psychopath Free website. It wasn't shame or anything like that. It was just strange to share this private part of my life with the rest of the world. But the more I started talking about it, the easier it got.

As you become your most genuine self, the people around you will not-so-coincidentally start to transform as well. Enjoy this, and don't forget to credit yourself for all of the hard work you've done to make it a reality.

Discovering the Beauty We've Always Had

I've always been inspired by HealingJourney's writing, but this piece truly blew me away:

> *He thought of how he had been pursued and scorned, and now he heard them all say that he was the most beautiful of all beautiful birds. The lilacs bent their boughs right down into the water before him, and the bright sun was warm and cheering. He rustled his feathers and raised his slender neck aloft, saying with exultation in his heart, "I never dreamt of so much happiness when I was the Ugly Duckling!"*
>
> —"The Ugly Duckling," by Hans Christian Andersen

It is amazing how profoundly an encounter with a psychopath can change one's view of the world, including those things that have always been so familiar, such as the above fairy tale. Although I always liked "The Ugly Duckling" because it has a happy ending, it was not my favorite story because it made me inexplicably sad. I never explored *why* it made me sad; I think it was too painful for me to do that then. But after going through such a dark time, I know I was sad because I saw myself for so long as the ugly duckling. I never imagined I could transform myself into a beautiful swan. Ironically, this horrible trauma has given me the opportunity to do just that. It has taken time and many stumbles, but I see the significant beauty within me now. I see myself as the swan, and I feel a wonderful sense of belonging. I am able to rejoice in my own uniqueness! That beauty is inside *every* survivor, a beauty we have possessed all along and never knew we had. As you make your way through your own recovery journey, you have the power to discover the beauty within by seeing and accepting the following truths:

You were not stupid; you were innocent.

When you first realized the extent of the psychopath's betrayal, you probably were overwhelmed by shame. How is it that you did not see the extent of the lies and the manipulation? It is normal to feel so very stupid when reality sinks in. And it is easy to become angry with yourself for not realizing that the "love" the psychopath offered you was an illusion. This is exactly how the psychopath—master of deception—wants you to feel, yet it is not the truth! You are a loving, empathetic person. You were never taught that emotionally crippled human predators are out there; you only heard about them in fairy tales or in stories of serial killers. You did not know that they walk among us, many of them seemingly normal, law-abiding citizens. You cannot protect yourself from something that you never knew existed. The ugly duckling simply did not know that he was always a swan and never a duck. He should not be blamed for his innocence, and neither should you.

It is okay to have insecurities and vulnerabilities.

You have probably been warned that it is "bad" to be insecure or vulnerable. You may even be taught this by those who are attempting to help you heal from psychopathic abuse. Yet struggling with insecurities and being vulnerable with others are part of what makes you a normal human being. Even the most confident people doubt themselves at times; even the most emotionally healthy people need to open up their hearts to others *and become vulnerable,* if they want to build intimate, meaningful relationships. It is absolutely possible for you to gain new confidence and still retain the ability to allow others—the *right* others—into your inner circle. The ugly duckling decided to trust a man who found him half frozen in the snow, and he was nurtured back to health. He allowed himself to be vulnerable, even after all of the taunting and abuse he endured. You can do the same thing; and you should do it carefully and based on what you have learned from your experiences.

Your weaknesses *and* strengths were exploited.

You may feel that the ways in which you were used by the psychopaths only showcase your shortcomings. You may believe that you have unique problems that make you a psychopath magnet. You were too trusting, you lacked boundaries, you did not love yourself enough, and so on. It is certainly true that your weaknesses were exploited. But your strengths were *also* exploited. The ability to love is a strength. The ability to trust is a strength. The ability to cooperate is a strength. The ability to be kind and honest and empathetic is a strength.

A psychopath has no conscience, and because of that, he or she is capable of horrific cruelty. He or she uses pity plays to capitalize on your natural desire to offer kindness and understanding. The psychopath mirrors your values and all aspects of your personality—including your positive qualities—in order to make you believe that he or she is just like you, when in fact he or she is the opposite. The psychopath sets you up in such a way that you project your own goodness onto him or her. The ugly duckling hoped that the woman, cat, and hen he turned to for help would be as kind as he was, and he unfortunately was wrong. But that did not take away from his wonderful qualities. And in your case, being targeted by a psychopath does not mean there is anything wrong with you.

Facing the pain sets you free.

In the aftermath, after you free yourself from the psychopathic bond, you are left traumatized. You are like the ugly duckling, frozen in the winter landscape. You are numb, confused, left in a fog, and you are battling very intense pain. You desperately want the pain to end, and you often do whatever you can to run away from it.

Avoidance and denial are normal, natural human responses to pain. All normal human beings do both, to varying degrees and for varying lengths of time. However, when you find the courage inside you to really face the pain and work through it, that is when you find freedom from the pain. That is when you experience new and life-changing joy. You cannot circle around the pain and discover the happiness you deserve. You must travel through the pain and embrace all of the challenging feelings and difficult ups and downs that are the essence of the grieving process. For a long time, it may seem as if you will always be hurting . . . until one day you will find that you turned a corner and found a lovely new world you never could have imagined.

When you embrace the above truths, you find who you are at a deeper level. And you realize that you have the ability to transform yourself in ways that psychopaths never can. You realize that the beauty within you has *always* been there. You can grow and change and evolve into the special and wonderful human being you always were and always were meant to be. You have the opportunity to develop new wisdom, to embrace a new vision, and use both to find the inner light that was hidden within you and allow that light to shine. And when you do, you will learn how to trust yourself again, and you will find other people who appreciate you and love you.

"He felt quite glad of all the misery and tribulation he had gone through, for he was the better able to appreciate his good fortune now and all the beauty which greeted him. The big swans swam round and round him and stroked him with their bills."

The ugly duckling found his way home, and you will, too.

Thirty Signs of Strength

Dreamers are eternal optimists. We want to believe the best in everything and everyone around us. This is a blessing, but it can also become a trap when toxic people are involved. The problem is that we begin to ignore and excuse their unacceptable behavior in order to maintain our unconditional faith in them. We fear that voicing our concerns makes these concerns real, and somehow destroys the dream. And so we choose to focus only on the positives. But eventually, everyone has a breaking point—when our boundaries have been violated too many times. So we react, and suddenly we become Enemy Number One. How dare you stop being a doormat? How could you betray them by suddenly no longer excusing all of their abuse? Additionally, onlookers will be quick to point out how highly you always spoke about this person, so why the sudden change of heart? And that is how dreamers become trapped in relationships with parasites. Abusers and spectators will not blame the abuse itself—instead, they will blame your newfound reactions to the abuse. You are always expected to remain cheerful and positive. But around toxic people, this isn't sustainable. And even if you do get people to understand that you're the victim, that you're being abused, it all becomes your fault. A lot of people hear the words "relationship abuse" and immediately think of weakness and vulnerability. This is an unfortunate social stigma, because the reality is that *anyone* can fall prey to a psychopath. In fact, psychopaths pride themselves on grooming and tearing down strong, successful targets. So whether you're cheerful, insecure, happy, sad, popular, lonely, confident, self-conscious, emotional, reserved, funny, shy, awkward, or any combination of the above—it makes no difference.

Nobody deserves to be abused.

The truth is, it is not your weaknesses that they target—it is your strengths. And what I've found is that the psychopathic experience actually endows you with even more strengths. And it will be these strengths that will enable you to heal and move forward—whole, confident, and with love.

I've met some of my best friends through Psychopath Free, and I have come to discover some qualities in these friends that I believe to be universal among many survivors:

1. **Actions over words.** Healthy, humble individuals do not constantly talk about the good things they have done, because it would be arrogant and uncomfortable. Instead, they prove it through their actions.

2. **Strong moral compass.** Survivors have always paid strong attention to rules and ethics. They are frightened of getting into trouble at school, or breaking the law, or hurting a

romantic partner. Their happiness does not infringe upon the happiness of others, and they strive to see that same good in others.

3. **Take responsibility for their actions.** Instead of blaming others for their problems, they tend to take full responsibility. They are not looking for excuses or scapegoats.

4. **Gentle and compassionate.** Survivors tend to be the type of people who are always willing to compromise and make things better. They are approachable, warm, and sensitive to the feelings of others.

5. **Apologize when the situation calls for it.** Will always say "sorry" when they do something wrong (and sometimes even when they haven't done anything wrong at all). While manipulators will only apologize if they can get something out of it, their targets apologize in order to restore peace and trust.

6. **Idealistic, romantic, and imaginative.** Survivors are often creators—artists, writers, spiritual workers, and musicians. These dreamer types may find it more difficult than most to reconcile their ideals with reality, but a world without dreamers would be very sad indeed.

7. **Dislike of conflict and criticism.** Psychopaths seek out people who will not stand up to them. This doesn't mean submissive and weak. It means conflict-averse, and willing to set aside issues in order to maintain harmony. Survivors make great colleagues and roommates!

8. **Optimism.** This is what can make it so difficult for a victim to leave their abuser. They continue to hope that things will change and go back to the way they were in the idealization phase. They want to see the best in everyone, and the plus side of this is they help others see the best in themselves. Their optimism is contagious and they keep people hopeful.

9. **Forgiving.** Although they have a hard time forgiving themselves, most survivors tend to be very forgiving when it comes to someone else's wrongdoings. They don't judge and they don't hold grudges.

10. **Always strive to see the good in others.** They project their own good nature and conscience onto others, mostly because they want to see the inherent good in all people. Although part of recovery is learning to recognize people for who they actually are, whether those qualities be positive or negative, expecting the best in others actually makes (normal, empathetic) people be their best.

11. **Naturally understand the insecurities of others.** Survivors seem to have some sort of "autodetect" mode for the soft spots in others. Once these qualities are noted, survivors are intuitively aware of how to approach those vulnerabilities with respect and kindness (as opposed to over-the-top flattery offered by psychopaths).

12. **Strive for win/win situations.** Conflict is inevitable when it comes to relationships, family, and work, but empathetic people are naturally prone to seek out solutions that leave everyone feeling happy.

13. **Understand and appreciate others' need for space.** Survivors can usually tell when someone needs time alone, as opposed to offering extra attention or cheering up. They are not smothering or overbearing, and instead tend to be strong listeners who can sense when they are needed.

14. **Flexible and easygoing.** They can adapt to most any situation, especially if it's for someone they care about. Very low maintenance when it comes to relationships, and unlikely to point out inappropriate behavior until their boundaries have been repeatedly violated. Even when warranted, they will likely feel bad after reprimanding someone else.

15. **Focus on the positive.** They see the best in others and in situations, emphasizing the good and not getting bogged down in the negative details.

16. **Unusual level of respect and loyalty for their partners.** They are committed to proving loyalty and building trust at all times. No matter what challenges might occur in the relationship, they will be determined to treat their partner well.

17. **Associate sex with emotions, not as a purely physical act.** Sex entails strong feelings and bonds. Survivors prefer becoming comfortable and intimate with one partner, as opposed to a never-ending string of casual encounters.

18. **Seek out lifelong partners.** Going along with the above point, most survivors are on a quest to find a long-term

romantic partner—not just dating and flings. Even in the early stages of the relationship, they might be assessing various qualities in their partner to determine if things would work out in the future.

19. **Self-deprecating and humble.** They don't feel any need to present an inflated or impressive version of themselves, because it's far easier to feel comfortable around modest people.

20. **Feel the greatest degree of happiness when making others happy.** Survivors are driven by an innate desire to make others open up, laugh, and feel good about themselves. A simple smile from a stranger can boost their entire day.

21. **Warmly enthusiastic about animals and/or children.** Total respect and admiration for the inherent innocence in others.

22. **Justice-driven.** Survivors tend to be truth seekers who can't fully relax until they understand every experience that shapes them. Shrugging and saying "well, life just sucks" isn't a valid option.

23. **Value opinions, ideas, and beliefs of others.** Even when they disagree with others, they never resort to mocking or dismissing someone else's core beliefs. Their friends and partners are not nervous to be open and honest about their true feelings, because they'll always be met with an open mind (as long as the ideas are presented in a respectful way).

24. **Hidden strength.** Surprising contrast between apparent submissiveness and actual strength. Survivors have a deep resilience that sustains them.

25. **Hardworking and independent.** Survivors work hard in every aspect of their life—whether it be at work, in the family, or helping others on the forum. In fact, I've never met so many motivated people in my life as I have on the website. Nobody wants to be the victim or permanently suffer from their past.

26. **Good listening skills.** A lot of people are always waiting for you to finish talking so they can start their own story. Survivors will spend hours listening to others, and are able to empathize without relating everything back to themselves.

27. **Able to enjoy time alone.** Not easily bored and seeking out constant thrills. This doesn't mean unadventurous. It means appreciating consistency and reliability in their core relationships. They don't need external stimulation every day in order to be happy, and they actually sometimes require time on their own to recharge.

28. **Polite to complete strangers.** You've probably heard of the "waiter test," where you can gauge a lot of things about your date based on how they treat the waiter at a restaurant. I think this is actually an incredibly effective way to measure a person's moral compass. Malcolm Forbes expressed this same thought when he said, "You can easily judge the character of a man by how he treats those who can do nothing for him."

29. **Connected with nature.** Enjoy time outside, getting in touch with the world around them. Respect trees, animals, flowers, plants, and everything else Mother Nature has to offer. Uplifted by a sunny day, and awestruck by the power of a thunderstorm.

30. **Lifelong quest for harmony, peace, and love.** Every survivor I've ever encountered is on their own path to freedom. However they choose to accomplish this, I will always have the utmost admiration and respect for their resiliency and their drive to turn darkness into light. This—in my opinion—is the most magical of all human qualities.

I bet you see a lot of these traits in yourself. You should respect and celebrate these qualities and seek them out in others.

Instead of beating yourself up for "losing" the psychopath's game, remember that they were seeking to win by destroying those qualities in you—qualities they will never have. They tried to trick you into believing that there is something wrong with all of those things, turning your beautiful strengths into unattractive flaws. But guess what? They didn't destroy those qualities—you still have them inside you. And now that you recognize their value you can go back to being your true, authentic self—the beautiful, loving, empathetic individual who brightens the world.

At the beginning of this book, I shared the Thirty Red Flags of a Psychopath—signs to look out for in manipulative and abusive individuals. Perhaps now you can use these thirty signs of strength as a guide to recognize empathetic people, the kind of people you want in your life. You want someone who seeks peace and harmony instead of drama. You want someone who is kind, compassionate, and loyal. You want someone who listens to you, values you, and sees the best in you. And you want the optimist, the romantic, the dreamer. There are so many other dreamers out there, just like you. And once you find them, you'll never look back.

Spirituality and Love

Psychopathic relationships are characterized by fantasy beginnings, quickly followed by identity erosion and cold-blooded devastation. Unlike the honeymoon phase experienced in many healthy relationships, a predator's love-bombing does not slowly settle into a more normal equilibrium. Their behavior rapidly oscillates from one unhealthy extreme to the other. Your partner will go from enthusiastically planning marriage and children to suddenly criticizing your body and calling you crazy.

Most survivors find that their lives are relatively stable when the psychopath arrives—a steady job, decent friends, and everyday insecurities. But after a few months, all of this is destroyed. Savings lost, fights with friends, and mind-boggling insecurities. Your comfortable life transforms into a nightmare of desperation and uncertainty. You take uncharacteristic risks for the "soul mate" who once swept you off your feet, only to find that they are treating you worse than ever before. And when all is said and done, it will seem that you have lost everything, in exchange for nothing.

These relationships leave survivors feeling drained and depleted of their life force.

Through the recovery process, we build ourselves back up from total darkness. From emptiness and hopelessness, we discover qualities in ourselves that we never valued before: creativity, kindness, humility, compassion. The foundation of our very spirits. As we work to become our most genuine selves, psychopaths continue their cycles of abuse forever and always, like twisted clockwork. They are incapable of growth and change, which is why they despise the people they attempt to destroy. But the human spirit cannot be destroyed, and this is why psychopaths will always fail—time after time after time after time.

Once you have self-respect, you are free to become who you were always meant to be. You do not care about the petty judgments of others, giving you the opportunity to fully explore your creativity, imagination, and spirituality.

This is where the magic begins.

Embrace the new you, and open your heart to love again. You should be so incredibly proud of yourself. You made it, and your life path has forever changed for the better. You might encounter toxic people, but you know you'll never fall for one again. Your mind, heart, and body have all aligned, rendering you invincible to the mind games of the soulless.

You no longer waste your time ruminating on the past because the present and future are so much brighter. Instead of analyzing the ambiguous behavior of others, you stop yourself immediately and simply remove them from your life. You know better now.

Your spirit wakes up after years of hibernation, ready to take on the world and reconnect with this great universe. You have an important place here, and you always have. You do things for you, not to impress others. Our friend MorningAfter wrote one of the most touching pieces I've ever seen. In my eyes, this is the true face of healing:

Slowly but Surely

I used to get into a panic if my phone didn't ring on weekends. Now I get into panic if it does.

I used to feel sad and lonely if I didn't go out—now I need more time alone because of so many books I want to read, things I want to do in my flat, hours I want to spend walking. My day needs to be longer.

I used to be so self-centered about how I looked that I used to wear uncomfortable shoes with high heels to go to work. Today I went to the office wearing flats and I felt good. Wearing high heels makes me feel better, but if I can't feel good with myself in old jeans, the best dress won't help me.

I used to wear makeup always, every day. Now it is not necessary. It's fun to put it on, but it's no longer a prerequisite for walking out the door.

I appreciate people smiling more than before. I feel more connected with people now than before. I see people walking and smiling and I spend a second thinking about them and I feel happy for them.

There is sadness also. But it is what life is made of. Both good and bad things. But how I feel them makes a difference.

My fear is that I will not make close friendships and close relationships anymore. But I've only walked one-third of the average recovery path so far, so who can know what waits for me in the future? I am afraid of relying on somebody . . . but the beauty I am discovering now is to rely on myself—for the very first time in my life. And to have a good time doing that.

Sometimes it appears to be lonely here where I am, but that conclusion is based upon my old type of thinking. I am not lonely, I just cleared out the miserable and mean people from my life, and I have space left for new good people and good things to come into my life.

Slowly but surely.

Gratitude and Forgiveness

During the healing process, we often lose sight of how much good there is in the world. But it is there, from the moment you wake up in the morning to the last thing you see before drifting off to sleep. All you have to do is open your heart to it.

Every day, amazing things are happening. People are laughing, birds flying, children playing, waves crashing . . . What an enchanting life this is! But when we spend time focusing on the very few things that aren't going well, we lose sight of what really matters—we forget how to be happy.

I would like to share a practice that has helped me cultivate gratitude over the past few years. It might not work for you, but it brings so much peace to my heart. Before going to sleep each night, I think about someone I am grateful for. It is usually my mom or a close friend. I imagine their face, their smile, and their genuine goodness.

I bow to their spirit, and then I repeat this process for another trusted spirit. And another. And another. I am always surprised to find that this activity never ends. I have never reached "the end" before falling asleep, because I do not believe there is an actual end to all the good people in this world.

Some survivors, myself included, place a great deal of importance in the idea of forgiveness. With the above activity, you can slowly start to integrate the people who have hurt you into your peaceful thoughts. It will feel wrong at first, and the very idea of them might trigger angry thoughts. But slowly, they will find a soft place in your heart. How could they not, when surrounded by so much love?

Do not mistake forgiveness for contact. Just because you forgive the psychopath does not mean they should ever have a place in your life again. And you certainly should not feel the need to tell them that you've forgiven them. True forgiveness comes from within, not from another person validating your compassion.

If you choose not to forgive the psychopath, that's fine, too. Some survivors feel that this would be an insult to their soul, and I completely understand. This is your decision, and I would never hope to understand the inner workings of someone else's heart. Do whatever brings you the most happiness—only you will know how to do that.

A Strange Conversation

We all have them. Self-doubts. Racing thoughts. Worries about ourselves, the future, and the world around us. This becomes especially and cripplingly true after relationship abuse.

When we're hurting, our immediate wish is that we'll stop hurting. I believe this is the mind's natural reaction to pain. We are self-healing beings, and so it only makes sense after an abusive relationship that we'd want to start feeling good again as soon as possible. But, as we all learn, it's not that easy. It takes years of recovery to dig deep, work hard, and reclaim our self-worth—to find our place and our confidence in this world.

And even then, the journey isn't over.

Years later—with self-respect, healthy relationships, and wonderful friendships—I began to notice this constant aching in my chest. I never seemed able to describe it quite right, but it was there with me every second of the day. Many survivors experience something similar, manifesting in a variety of different ways. Previously, I described it this way:

The demon that wraps its claws around your heart, always there to remind you of everything you want to forget.

I spent weeks of my life researching this demon, trying to figure out why it wouldn't leave me alone. I wanted so badly for it to go away, allowing me to enjoy life as I once remembered. I would try to convince myself that it had disappeared, even when I could feel it sneaking back up on me. I considered medications, although I avoided this route for personal reasons.

And then one day I came across a therapist who specialized in "Imagination Therapy." That sounded good to me. I love anything to do with creativity and the mind. So I met up with her and spent the next several weeks diving into my imagination.

I would like to share what I learned (along with some of my own inventions), in case it helps anyone who suffers from this lingering darkness. You are not alone, and you do not need to hurt like this anymore.

The first thing I needed to revisit was this idea of a "demon," which automatically implied that the dark feeling was my enemy. How could it not be, after all the time I had spent hating it and wishing it away? Fear is a powerful thing, and it keeps us strongly rooted in our distress.

But it's time to break that pattern of thinking. It's time for you to meet this darkness face-to-face.

Make sure you are somewhere relaxing. Bubble baths are my favorite. And then take several deep breaths: five seconds in through your nose. Hold for five seconds. Five seconds out through your mouth. Now become aware of the dark feeling as it starts to take over, even in this relaxing environment.

But today, instead of wishing it away, welcome it. It's scary, but I promise you will not be harmed. Welcome all of the racing thoughts, worries, doubts, and physical symptoms that come along with it. And once you are completely consumed . . .

Introduce yourself.

Below is my own personal recollection of the conversation that followed. It changed my life. And I hope it might serve as a guide for your own discoveries.

Unexpected Answers to Unexpected Questions: Why Are You Here?

I expected a nasty response, a distant voice from my ex telling me I deserved to suffer. That I was crazy, weak, and pathetic.

So you can imagine my surprise when he (yes, it was unmistakably a young boy) gently responded: "I'm here to make sure you're okay."

That changed everything. Suddenly he didn't seem so scary. But I still had to wonder why he was hurting me, keeping my chest so tight and uncomfortable. Answering before I could even ask, he said: "I've only been hugging your heart to keep you safe. I never meant for it to harm you."

And suddenly I didn't want this boy to leave me. Granted, I wished he'd stop hugging me so hard, but I wasn't afraid of him anymore. I trusted him very quickly. There was something loving, kind, and innocent about him. I wanted to learn more.

Forgotten Memories: When Did You Arrive?

I figured he must have joined me after the relationship. That's when I started feeling his "hugs," after all. So I asked how he found me, and why he decided to stay. Again, his answer surprised me.

He said that he'd been with me since the day I was born. He was my energy, my creativity—my living spirit. He would stay with me forever, and he was so excited that we were finally talking.

The hugs, however, were much more recent. I had never needed them in the past. I was a naturally cheerful person, and he could simply live and breathe through me. But when I was broken, he couldn't do that anymore. When I encountered evil, he was repeatedly silenced and shoved aside. Everything we once valued together was violated. And so he stayed with me, waiting quietly.

Patiently. He would do whatever it took to make sure that I'd never be treated so badly again.

In the meantime, he did everything in his power to sabotage my relationship. He refused to watch me submit to another human being. He lashed out when I wanted him to keep quiet. He was the one who couldn't stop pointing out the lies, hypocrisy, and manipulation—even though I tried so hard to ignore them, to maintain the idealization. He didn't care if I was called crazy or hypersensitive. He wanted me far and forever away from this black hole that consumed the both of us.

And finally, during the darkest moment of my life—when I considered leaving this world—he gave me a reason to stay here. He gave me hope.

A New Partnership: What Does the Future Hold?

I thanked him for protecting me. For keeping me safe. For seeing evil where I could not. But despite all of his unsung efforts, I needed him to understand that his hugs hurt me. I have learned and grown from my experience, and I promised him that I would never allow myself to be violated like that again. I asked if he could please just loosen his grip a bit.

He considered my proposal, and said he'd try his hardest. He told me that it would take time for him to let me go—that it wouldn't just happen overnight. He said that we would need to work together, to find a peaceful solution that worked for both of us. Of course I enthusiastically agreed. It was more progress than I'd made in two years.

I was able to say good night to him with a new kind of compassion. I went to sleep that night knowing that a loyal guardian was watching over my dreams, battling darkness with his eternal light and unconditional love.

My Weird Sunsets: Why Are We Here?

Since that night, I've had conversations with him every single day. He is my friend, and he has been with me since the very beginning—expecting nothing in return, just patiently waiting for that conversation. Whenever I begin to feel overwhelmed, I find that I can calm down quickly by simply saying: "Hey, what's going on?"

He always has an answer, and it's never a scary one.

I find that I connect best with him when I'm watching the sunset by the river. In these moments, I think I'm beginning to discover why we're all here on this strange planet. If we have these spirits within us, fighting for everything that is good, then surely they must be able to see and communicate with one another. Yours, mine, anyone's! I imagine they must enjoy playing together at night, laughing, crying, fighting, and protecting.

I am very touched by this gift, and I would not trade it for anything. This inner being—the very core of our true selves—has been with all of us since the day we entered this world. It cannot be destroyed, no matter how hard someone might try. Each and every one of us was violated in an incomprehensibly unfair way. We did not ask to have our innocence stolen from us. But in their attempts to destroy our identity, our predators only gave us the opportunity to connect even more deeply with our spirits.

And that is why psychopaths will always fail.

They do not understand love. They cannot feel anxiety and worry—these spirits within us, always making sure we are okay. They can mimic nearly anything else, but they cannot comprehend or experience the most important magic this world has to offer. Love is where the pitiful psychopathic games come to an end, and our journey only just begins.

Our spirits are here to help us, not to hurt us. They will always be ready for a conversation, excited to meet the people that they dedicate their lives to protecting. And until that conversation, they will be there for us: steadfast, strong, and ready for the next great adventure.

Finding Love Again

Surprisingly enough, love and sex after psychopathic recovery are better than ever before. Unlike anything you've ever experienced. You were originally conditioned to feel addicted to desperation and intense passion—something you once mistook for love. But now you know better. Love is gentle, patient, and kind. Love is consistent and creative. You do not doubt your partner's intentions. Instead, two spirits peacefully coexist, exploring the world together.

Depending on the degree and kind of abuse you suffered, you may need time to work through some sexual triggers. A truly good partner will give you all the time in the world. They will communicate and empathize, ensuring that you feel comfortable no matter what. Instead of sex being used for manipulation, you will find that normal, healthy partners have sex as a way to bond and express love for one another.

Once you're able to trust fully, your ability to experience physical and emotional intimacy will blossom like a flower—growing and maturing. You're finally able to apply all the things you've been learning throughout the healing process. You know what you deserve, and you know who you are. You are able to freely give your loving energy because it's respected and cherished, instead of being wasted on a black hole.

With psychopaths, you never know where you stand. You live in a constant state of uncertainty, wondering each day whether or not they care about you. Your entire life is consumed by this day-by-day struggle. But with real love, all of this garbage is forgotten. You do not question yourself. Your love is a mutual partnership of dedication and passion.

There is something truly amazing about meeting the right person and finally realizing, "Wow, they are never going to harm me." Think about that for a moment. You dealt with months—probably years—of emotional abuse, and now you've worked so hard that everything has changed. You ended the cycle of emotional violence, all on your own. You uprooted your patterns and redefined your life's path. And as a reward, your heart is finally free.

Do not worry about when this will happen. Maybe you're perfectly content without a partner, and that's wonderful. But for those of us seeking love, someone will come along and recognize all of the greatness within us. And what's more, you will know in your heart when you've found the one. There is no rush.

You know that feeling you get when you discover a great song and you listen to it on repeat all day, wondering how you ever went a day in your life without hearing it? Love is sort of like that. It pops up out of nowhere, and before you know it, you're singing along for the rest of your life.

The Fool & the World

The Fool turns to take that final step along his final path, and finds, to his bemusement, that he is right back where he started, at the edge of that very same cliff he almost stepped over when he was young and too foolish to look where he was going. But now he sees his position very differently. He thought he could separate body and mind, learn all about one, then leave it to learn about the other. But in the end, it is all about the self: mind and body, past and future, the individual, and the world. All one, including the Fool and the Mystic who are both doorways to the secrets of the universe. With a knowing smile, the Fool takes that final step right off the cliff . . . and soars. Higher and higher, until the whole of the world is his to see. And there he dances, surrounded by a yoni of stars, at one with the universe. Ending, in a sense, where he began, beginning again at the end. The world turns, and the Fool's journey is complete. (By Thirteen, Aeclectic Tarot, www.aeclectic.net)

Picture a twenty-one-year-old closeted gay virgin who's just starting to go through puberty, walking through campus to his computer-programming class in a pair of torn Walmart jeans.

That was me!

As you can probably imagine, I was the most insecure person on the planet. I was an awkward, acne-prone redhead who'd never had a boyfriend or a girlfriend—I'd never been seen as "attractive" by anybody. And so, my insecurities came mostly from my sexuality (or lack thereof). As shallow as it sounds, I was insecure about the way I looked. Of course, back then, I didn't know I was insecure, which is the most unfortunate kind of insecurity.

But that was only a small part of Jackson. Mostly I just liked to run around, be hyper, make friends, be happy, enjoy quiet time, and build cat houses. Nothing ever really bothered me, and I never held a grudge because it was a waste of energy. I liked making grumpy people happy—I thought that anything could be cured with a little bit of kindness. I loved to take people on adventures, and I dreamed about someday having a family and kids of my own.

All of those things together are what make a personality, but during the darkest time of my life, my insecurities took over and became my entire identity. All of the good things got pushed aside to make room for my faults, which became more pronounced as I spiraled deeper and deeper into a black hole.

And when the relationship came to an end, I decided that my entire old self must have been the root cause of everything. Instead of examining my insecurities one by one, I just tossed the whole personality away. I wanted to be someone new! What a lazy way to deal with my problems. And I paid the price for that. I lost a great job opportunity, freaked out at my friends, spent my life savings, moved into a fancy apartment, tried being a "tough guy," tried being sexy. It didn't work (especially that last part).

When I look back now, the strangest thing about this journey is that I really didn't come very far at all, linearly speaking. Most of my recovery was spent working my way back to the person I used to be, with a few small tweaks. I used to think I needed to uproot everything in order for my recovery to have meaning, but that wasn't the case at all. In fact, I was most unsettled when I tried to declare war on my old self and everything I used to value.

Maybe you had insecurities of your own, childhood traumas, secret vanities, bad relationships, or something else entirely. But no matter what struggles you faced, if you dig deep enough, I bet you'll come to see some really neat qualities in that person, too. On top of that, maybe you can learn to appreciate the fact that your old self was doing the best it could, given the circumstances.

Once we take on this more gentle view of our past selves, the whole recovery process seems to feel a lot more pleasant. Instead of this overwhelming, all-consuming character transformation, we're just introspecting a bit and learning to recognize the qualities that make us who we are—for better or for worse. It can be really disheartening to discover this at first, because it feels like you've already lost that old, trusting, loving spirit.

Well, there's good news and bad news here. The good news is that your "old self" didn't actually go anywhere. That wouldn't even make sense.

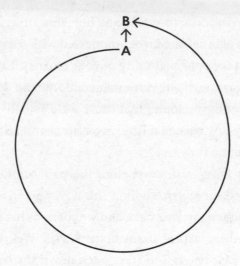

The bad news is that I made another chart in Microsoft Paint.

As you can see, there are two ways to get from Point A to Point B. You can either walk one centimeter upward, or you can take the obnoxiously long and roundabout way there.

The thing about life is that you're not aware that the short path exists until you've already taken the long path. People can tell you all about how to take the shortcut. You can read lots of books about how to take the shortcut. A parent can tell a child how to take the shortcut. People spend tons of money trying to find the shortcut. I've just *shown* you the shortcut in the form of a beautiful diagram. But none of that actually works. You will only see the shortcut after you've already walked the long path for yourself.

And that's a good thing! We learn so much when we take the long way. It's scary at first, but you'll soon find that there are so many mysteries and opportunities at every corner. With each step, you gain more and more perspective about yourself and the world. Some days feel miserable and hopeless, others feel promising and full of insights. Maybe you started with compassion and blind trust at the very beginning of your journey. Later, you decided those qualities made you a vulnerable human doormat. But closer to Point B, you found that those were actually wonderful things—they just needed a little awareness and self-respect in order to function fully.

Every tiny thing we discover along this path contributes to our perception and our understanding. This is why, when we get closer to our destination, we look back and wonder: "What the hell was I thinking—there were so many better ways!" Well, duh, in retrospect. It's easy enough to stare back down the shortcut and wonder how we missed it, but the only reason we're even able to judge ourselves like that is *because* of this long path we're walking—because of the mistakes, embarrassments, failures, and lessons learned.

The reason I love that quote about the Fool & the World is because he's still a Fool at the end of his journey. He's still the same person he always was, just with some newfound knowledge and wisdom picked up along the way.

So what's the lesson here? Well, my lesson was to go through puberty before age twenty-one next time. Yours is probably different, because we're all walking very different paths on that big circle—plus, I'm starting to suspect that Point B isn't even anywhere close to the end.

A Bigger Picture

Empathetic people—dreamers and idealists—have this sort of accidental power. Most spend their early years riddled with self-doubt, insecurity, and people-pleasing habits. But their journey is inevitably derailed when this comfortable life gets uprooted by an unexpected darkness. Suddenly their trusted methods no longer seem to bring them happiness. At first this depression convinces them that they might never feel joyful again. But ultimately, it sets them on a quest for something more—for love, justice, and wisdom. Once this adventure begins, there is no stopping a dreamer.

And when dreamers unite?

Well, that's how we start to change the world.

Families, the Workplace, and Society

While this book was written primarily for survivors of harmful romantic relationships, the psychopathic cycle of abuse is univer-

sal. It is characterized by intense idealization and personality mirroring, closely followed by devaluation and identity erosion. This
process is certainly not limited to romantic relationships, and
considering the high prevalence of Cluster B personality disorders,
chances are that you or someone you know has experienced this
in a boss, parent, sibling, friend, coworker, or neighbor.

In your family, you might have dealt with a parent who abused
you since childhood, using you merely as a tool to get what they
wanted from the rest of the world—having impossible expectations of you while realizing none of those expectations in their
own behavior. If you didn't adhere to their strict rules, you were
promptly punished with silence and ridicule, leaving you feeling
worthless and unloved. And just when you were feeling like you
couldn't take it anymore, they showered you with the praise and
admiration you so desperately craved. You were constantly walking on eggshells, your very foundation completely unstable. It
takes years of therapy and self-work to overcome such persistent
brainwashing.

At your job, you may have encountered a manipulative coworker who charmed their way into your professional life, only
to backstab you once they got what they needed. Whispering poison into everyone else's ears, their covert triangulation turned an
entire workplace against you. If you spoke up, you sounded crazy
because you were insulting everyone's favorite employee: the one
who was sweet to everybody (except you, behind closed doors).

And then there's the psychopath as boss. Their charismatic
qualities often allow them to work their way to the top pretty
quickly. They're the manager who has no problem abusing you
because they know you can't do anything about it. They give you

your paycheck, so you have to put up with anything they throw your way, otherwise you're fired. They spend the company's money irresponsibly, they discredit others, and they take down anyone who stands in their way. They're a bully and a manipulator, but somehow they always appear to be the innocent one.

There is this strange idea floating around that psychopaths can be useful, perhaps even necessary, in the workplace—that they're able to make the tough decisions no one else can make. But anyone who has actually dealt with a psychopath at work will dismiss this in a heartbeat. Psychopaths wreak havoc, cause irreparable damage, and can destroy an office's entire culture from the inside out. They manage to do all of this while appearing completely innocent and placing the blame on someone else. They have no problem ruining a coworker's or subordinate's life in order to advance their own career. In fact, they look forward to doing it.

And if that's not frightening enough, consider that these people are pathologically attracted to power, money, and crime. From Dr. Robert Hare's work, we already know that psychopaths make up an unusually high percentage of the prison population. But what about the vast majority of psychopaths who are not incarcerated? Where do they end up?

Wall Street? Washington, D.C.?

These are places where backstabbing and dishonesty aren't just acceptable—they're expected. Politicians charm their way into power with charisma and rosy promises, only to leave us feeling angry when they use their position to accomplish the polar opposite. This behavior has become so commonplace that political promises are now nothing more than material for late-night comedians. But it's not very funny at all. It's actually quite scary.

We find ourselves regularly betrayed by our elected politicians, but we have come to believe that this sort of behavior is normal. We believe that it is normal for full-grown adults to behave like manipulative children, for politicians to make promises they never intend to keep, and for governments to spit on the very same documents they are sworn to uphold.

But it is not normal. This is not political theater. This is not power corrupting once-decent men and women.

This is the Cluster B disorders in action.

This is what happens when parasites infest a strong, successful nation of idealists and dreamers. This is what happens when toxic people are attracted to power and understand how to obtain it. This is what happens when our leaders are hypocrites who feel entitled to stomp on standards they were elected to enforce.

Psychopaths cause damage wherever they go. In struggling to understand an abusive partner, a conniving coworker, a manipulative parent, or even pathological leadership, we're all seeking a very similar path to freedom. First, we must understand that there are people who walk this world completely devoid of conscience and empathy.

And then, much more importantly, we learn to value these qualities in ourselves.

The 15 Percent Problem

There are more sociopaths among us than people who suffer from the much-publicized disorder of anorexia, four times as many sociopaths as schizophrenics, and one hundred times as

many sociopaths as people diagnosed with a known scourge
such as colon cancer.

—Dr. Martha Stout, *The Sociopath Next Door*

Numbers are usually sort of tedious to me, but I think these are worth examining.

According to the National Institutes of Health:

- 6 percent of the general population has narcissistic personality disorder (NPD).
- 5 percent of the general population has borderline personality disorder (BPD).
- 2 percent of the general population has histrionic personality disorder (HPD).

And according to Dr. Martha Stout:

- 4 percent of the general population has antisocial personality disorder (ASPD, sociopathy, or psychopathy).

These are the Cluster B personality disorders, and based on the statistics above, they are found in more than one in every seven people—over 15 percent of the population (I'm rounding down, to account for comorbidity). Now consider that most of these people are highly functional, nonincarcerated, active members of society. So given the raw numbers, it's highly likely that you unknowingly pass by one of these cunning manipulators every day on your way to work—perhaps even today, when they served you your morning coffee.

So what's the problem?

The problem is that the general public knows virtually nothing about these incredibly pervasive disorders. If you were to ask your friends what borderline personality disorder is, how many of them would have an answer? And how many of them would have an accurate answer?

Likewise, is someone with narcissistic personality disorder really just a person who looks in the mirror too much? And is someone with histrionic personality disorder really just a person who seeks out lots of attention?

You'd probably find that most people have heard of psychopathy, but how about psychopathy outside of serial killers and *Criminal Minds*? What about the far more common everyday social predator who charms and manipulates their way into someone's life? What about the chameleon who destroys an unsuspecting victim from the inside out, all the while appearing completely innocent?

The Cluster B disorders are disorders of emotion, conscience, empathy, and feeling—arguably some of the most important human qualities. So why are we not taught about these disorders in school? How have they received so little public attention?

Again, more than 15 percent of our population (I'm going to keep repeating that number) is made up of people with a severe and incurable emotional disorder—and yet, due to the hidden nature of their symptoms, we know practically nothing about them. Usually by the time someone decides to learn about personality disorders, the damage has already been done.

So how do we identify them before it's too late?

The four Cluster B disorders comprise various symptoms, but

they all have one thing in common: unhealthy, inappropriate, shallow, or completely nonexistent human emotions. These can manifest differently across each individual and disorder, but for their victims, the experience is universal: idealization and devaluation. People with Cluster B disorders are incapable of forming natural bonds with others, and as a result, they attempt to mimic this bond (whether it be intentional or not) through a "mean and sweet" cycle.

This book is written for survivors of these traumatic encounters, so that they might start to find answers and regain their sanity. I don't focus too much on the nitpicky differences between each disorder, because the impact on survivors of Cluster B disorders is always the same: confusion, hopelessness, and total emotional devastation.

When we understand that there are people who do not experience the world the way we do, everything finally starts to fall into place. Once we stop projecting our own conscience and inherent goodness onto everyone else, these inexplicable experiences begin to make perfect sense. For many of us, these disorders are a missing puzzle piece that will transform our entire lives.

Beyond the Thirty Red Flags, here's a brief overview of the four disorders:

Narcissistic Personality Disorder

In order for a person to be diagnosed with narcissistic personality disorder, the *DSM-IV-TR* states that they must meet five or more of the following symptoms:

- Expects to be recognized as superior and special, without superior accomplishments.
- Expects constant attention, admiration, and positive reinforcement from others.
- Envies others and believes others envy him/her.
- Is preoccupied with thoughts and fantasies of great success, enormous attractiveness, power, intelligence.
- Lacks the ability to empathize with the feelings or desires of others.
- Is arrogant in attitudes and behavior.
- Has expectations of special treatment that are unrealistic.

In their interpersonal relationships, this leads to early idealization in the honeymoon phase, where they groom you to become a constant source of positive energy—temporarily satisfying their pathological desire for admiration. But because they are also jealous and arrogant, you quickly start to discover that there won't be any room for your own happiness. Once you fail to meet their rapidly shifting standards, you will be devalued and criticized until you have nothing left to offer. The stark contrast between the idealization and devaluation leaves you feeling worthless, broken, and confused.

Borderline Personality Disorder

In order for a person to be diagnosed with borderline personality disorder, the *DSM-IV-TR* states that they must meet five or more of the following symptoms:

- Frantic efforts to avoid real or imagined abandonment.
- A pattern of unstable and intense interpersonal relationships *characterized by alternating between extremes of idealization and devaluation* [italics added].
- Identity disturbance: markedly and persistently unstable self-image or sense of self.
- Impulsivity in at least two areas that are potentially self-damaging (e.g., spending, sex, substance abuse, reckless driving, binge eating).
- Recurrent suicidal behavior, gestures, or threats, or self-mutilating behavior.
- Affective instability due to a marked reactivity of mood (e.g., intense episodic dysphoria, irritability, or anxiety usually lasting a few hours and only rarely more than a few days).
- Chronic feelings of emptiness.
- Inappropriate, intense anger or difficulty controlling anger (e.g., frequent displays of temper, constant anger, recurrent physical fights).
- Transient, Stress-Related Paranoid Ideation or Severe Dissociative Symptoms.

In their interpersonal relationships, this leads to early idealization in the honeymoon phase, where they groom you to become a constant source of positive energy—temporarily satisfying their pathological feelings of emptiness. But because they are also angry and impulsive, you quickly start to discover that there won't be any room for your own happiness. Once you fail to meet their rapidly shifting standards, you will be devalued and criticized until you have nothing left to offer to them. The stark contrast between the idealization and devaluation leaves you feeling worthless, broken, and confused.

Histrionic Personality Disorder

In order for a person to be diagnosed with histrionic personality disorder, the *DSM-IV-TR* states that they must meet five or more of the following symptoms:

- Is uncomfortable in situations in which he or she is not the center of attention.
- Interaction with others is often characterized by inappropriate sexually seductive or provocative behavior.
- Displays rapidly shifting and shallow expression of emotions.
- Consistently uses physical appearance to draw attention to self.
- Has a style of speech that is excessively impressionistic and lacking in detail.
- Shows self-dramatization, theatricality, and exaggerated expression of emotion.
- Is suggestible, i.e., easily influenced by others or circumstances.
- Considers relationships to be more intimate than they actually are.

In their interpersonal relationships, this leads to early idealization in the honeymoon phase, where they groom you to become a constant source of positive energy—temporarily satisfying their pathological need for attention. But because they are also provocative and exaggerated, you quickly start to discover that there won't be any room for your own happiness. Once you fail to meet their rapidly shifting standards, you will be devalued and criticized until you have nothing left to offer to them. The stark contrast between the idealization and devaluation leaves you feeling worthless, broken, and confused. (Do you see where I'm going with this?)

Antisocial Personality Disorder

In order for a person to be diagnosed with antisocial personality disorder, the *DSM-IV-TR* states that they must meet three or more of the following symptoms:

- Failure to conform to social norms with respect to lawful behaviors as indicated by repeatedly performing acts that are grounds for arrest.
- Manipulativeness: frequent use of subterfuge to influence or control others; use of seduction, charm, glibness, or ingratiation to achieve one's ends.
- Deceitfulness, as indicated by repeated lying, use of aliases, or conning others for personal profit or pleasure.
- Impulsivity or failure to plan ahead.
- Irritability and aggressiveness, as indicated by repeated physical fights or assaults.
- Reckless disregard for safety of self or others.
- Consistent irresponsibility, as indicated by repeated

failure to sustain consistent work behavior or honor financial obligations.

- Lack of remorse, as indicated by being indifferent to or rationalizing having hurt, mistreated, or stolen from another.

Drum roll, please . . . In their interpersonal relationships, this leads to early idealization in the honeymoon phase, where they groom you to become a constant source of positive energy—temporarily satisfying their pathological desire to charm and control others. But because they are also remorseless and deceitful, you quickly start to discover that there won't be any room for your own happiness. Once you fail to meet their rapidly shifting standards, you will be devalued and criticized until you have nothing left to offer to them. The stark contrast between the idealization and devaluation leaves you feeling worthless, broken, and confused.

Sorry for being redundant, but at 15 percent of the population, I think these things are worth repeating. If someone's opinion of you goes from sky-high to rock bottom, this isn't normal. When you first meet someone with a Cluster B personality disorder, it'll seem that all of your dreams have finally come true. They'll shower you with praise and apparent love, focusing all of their energy on you. It starts to feel like you're the only person in the world.

But, as you can see from the symptoms described above, this idealization is not at all genuine. It is based on a pathological need for something: whether it be admiration, filling the emptiness, attention, or control. The bottom line is, the idealization is certainly not based on *your* own unique qualities, because with Cluster B disorders, you are not viewed as a human being with feelings—you are viewed as a way to fill whatever emotional deficiency their disorder entails. Similar to brainwashing behavior by cults, the idealization is simply an artificial way to secure your trust and love so that you will ultimately become a reliable source of nourishment for their pathological needs.

Once you fail to meet their impossible and impulsive demands, your dream quickly shifts into a nightmare, where you feel constantly on edge and unable to express yourself. Every attempt at compassion and empathy falls on deaf ears—none of your usual interpersonal strategies seem to work anymore. You genuinely begin to believe that you are crazy, even though you've never felt this way until this person entered your life. Your old cheerful self rapidly dissolves into a paranoid mess of anxiety, desperation, and obsession.

This is abusive and destructive, and I believe something needs to change.

Everyone has different opinions on *what* needs to change. As awareness continues to spread, we see people with these personality disorders complaining that they shouldn't be discriminated against, because they have no choice in the matter—just like skin color or sexual orientation. Well, the difference is that skin color doesn't cause one person to erode another's identity. People with different skin colors aren't inherently more prone to harm others. Gay people aren't hardwired to manipulate their partners.

This is what makes the Cluster B disorders such a unique and sensitive topic. They allow a person to appear completely healthy and loving (oftentimes more so than a nondisordered individual), and the person uses this facade of normalcy to cause harm to anyone unfortunate enough to cross his or her path.

This is a problem posed by no other mental or physical ailment.

Some may be drawn to "help" or "heal" these people. I'm going to be blunt: this is not my concern. There are psychologists and scientists out there working really hard to understand and treat these disorders. But for now, they remain incurable, untreatable, and widespread.

So given the problem at hand, what can the rest of us do to protect ourselves?

I think the first step is education: getting the word out there. Helping people see that most psychopaths aren't Ted Bundy. Calling out toxic, manipulative behavior for what it really is. Illustrating the differences between calculated flattery and healthy, genuine love.

The next step is validation: helping victims through the darkness and showing them that they are not alone. Sharing experiences with one another and understanding how we were manipulated. At first, your personal story might feel too crazy for words. But that's always the case with Cluster B encounters. With the right key words and labels, you'll suddenly find millions of people who have gone through identical nightmares.

Next up is healing: shifting the focus from the abuser to the abused. Understanding what you truly lost from this experience, and much more importantly, what can be gained. Forming healthy boundaries and finding self-respect. Examining your own insecurities and vulnerabilities so that you can ultimately seek out happier, healthier relationships.

The final step is freedom: once you are able to identify and recognize toxic people, you realize that nothing can be gained from interacting with them. Instead of trying to fix broken people, you devote your valuable energy to equally empathetic friends and partners. No matter what they might promise, those with Cluster B disorders cannot and will not change for you.

Once these steps are in place, we have small ways of dealing with big problems. Our freedom allows us to live a life safe from harm in our interpersonal relationships. But what happens when we take a step back and look at the bigger picture—at our society, corporations, and culture . . . Exactly how much damage has the 15 percent caused?

We have a problem, that's for sure. But I am an optimist—and we optimists have our own screwed-up need to find solutions.

What Happens Next?

As unlikely as this might sound, somewhere down the road, I promise that your encounter with a psychopath won't really enter your mind anymore. You'll look back on it as a strange time that almost seems unreal in retrospect. Instead of being intense and overwhelming, it settles into a safe place in your heart and quietly becomes something good. This is the point at which we often see survivors say farewell to the forum, which always makes me sad and happy. Sad to see a friend go, of course—but far more happy to see a survivor excited to go out and explore a new life.

Everyone's going to have a different journey after healing from a psychopathic encounter. Some want to move on with their lives and never hear about a personality disorder again. Some choose to stick around and help other survivors through the darkness. And then there are those who slowly transform their own personal encounter into a much broader understanding of how empathy and conscience impact our world.

It all comes back to that 15 percent problem.

Once we've experienced the idealization and devaluing cycle for ourselves, we come to recognize it in various other aspects of life. From abusive partners to corporate manipulators to the lying politicians who run this world, we've reached a breaking point. It is not possible to coexist with people who actively seek to harm and control others. Evil isn't some sort of obscure concept anymore—it has a name. And because of that name, a skyrocketing number of us have already joined together and elucidated what once seemed inexplicable.

But at 15 percent of the general population, statistics would indicate that we've barely even scratched the surface. There are many millions more out there who still need answers—gentle, kind, good people who have been taught to doubt their greatest qualities. Dreamers who are one simple word away from finding freedom and transforming their entire lives.

Since the very beginning of our mission, our goal has been to reach these dreamers. It frustrates and saddens me to think of all the decent people who fall prey to these manipulative encounters every single day. And there's nothing I can do about it. Sure, we do our best to spread awareness, but that's mostly reaching people who've already gone far enough along the path to search for sociopaths, narcissists, manipulators, or something like that.

Those survivors are the rare exception.

What about the vast majority of people who don't even know

what they've just encountered? What about the people still stuck in the vicious cycle of idealization and devaluation? What about the people living the nightmare, instead of recovering from it? What about the people who still seek out destructive relationships, years after their original victimizing, because they don't know they were in an abusive relationship to begin with? What about the people who still desperately try to reason and empathize with someone who is psychologically incapable of returning the favor?

This book is my attempt at making a small difference, but the problem is huge.

There are seven billion people in the world. One in seven of those people is hardwired to manipulate, exploit, idealize, and devalue other human beings. I'm no good at math, but I'm pretty sure that comes out to one billion people with a Cluster B disorder.

Now consider that those one billion people are serial daters, chronic job hoppers, nonincarcerated criminals, and ruthless power seekers. They are in constant search of new victims, jumping from one source to the next with unrivaled haste. It would seem that the minority of the population is causing a hugely disproportionate number of problems in the world.

So what are the rest of us supposed to do?

If you ask me, I believe there's a battle on the horizon. Not the kind with guns and bombs—but instead, a battle of the human conscience. Throughout history, people have told stories of villains. From fairy tales to pop music to drawings in caves, they are all describing the same phenomenon: a battle between psychopaths and dreamers.

We've seen battles on nearly every other human quality imaginable: skin color, sexuality, gender, ethnicity . . . the list goes on.

After decades of hard work from human rights activists, people finally stop being idiots and come to understand that none of those things has anything to do with a person's character. So why in the world do we keep wasting our time inventing pointless witch hunts, when there are a billion people out there who *actually* cause harm to others?

There is so much at stake here: the very future of empathy, compassion, and love as we know it. Are these qualities strengths or weaknesses? Is the human conscience a brilliant evolutionary step for mankind, or is it a convenient vulnerability to be exploited?

There is a part of me that would love to move up to the mountains and never hear the word "psychopath" again—and I'm sure I'll do that someday. But for now, another part of me knows, deep down, that this is the most important issue of our time. There is so much beauty and magic in this world worth fighting for.

What happens next is up to us.

Afterword

The Constant: Revisited

What an adventure this has been. I'm sitting here with three cats and a hot cup of coffee, wondering why it took me so long to mention my cats. Sometimes they are my Constant. Sometimes my mom is my Constant. Sometimes memories from the beach are my Constant. Sometimes the members of Psychopath Free are my Constant.

It would seem that everyone in my life has become a Constant.

But back to my cats. I like to go for winter walks in the snow with them. They're weird, sort of like dogs, following the tracks I make out in the woods. Earlier this morning, we spent a long time out there, exploring and dreaming together. We discovered new and untold secrets of the universe. We learned about growing up and trusting love again. We found hope in the goodness of mankind. We saw Light and Dark, battling each other throughout all of eternity.

It was in that moment that I realized something: I am my own Constant. I love my quiet time alone. I love existing here in this mysterious world. I love being a part of something so much bigger than myself. And I love not having a clue what comes next.

But above all, I love that adversity has introduced me to some of the most incredible human beings this world has to offer. There is something connecting all of us, I am sure of it. And because of the friendships, I would not change my experience. Not in a million years.

Our adventure is only just beginning—and now that our hearts have healed, it's time to make some trouble. Or at least, that's what the cats are telling me.

Acknowledgments

I'm not sure who would actually want their name linked to a book about psychopaths, but these are the people who make my heart light up.

The Forum People

Smitten Kitten, for being an amazing friend and walking this weird road with me since the very beginning. Peru, for dreaming up Psychopath Free, and for always making us laugh. Victoria, for being your compassionate self in a million places all at once. HealingJourney, for your beautiful writing and friendship, and your hawk eyes! An Old-Fashioned Girl, for the ice skating and hugs. Iris, for helping so many families out of the darkness. MorningAfter, for working hard to change the world. Rydia, for all of the coffee and wine and editing and giggles. LuckyLaura, for being so ridiculously fun to chat with all day long. Indie917, for your wonderful intuition and sense of humor. Indie Mom, for giving hope and resources to families everywhere. OutOfTheAshes, for the hilarious things you say that I can't repeat here. Barberable, for your bravery so early on, and for your magical creativity. Phoenix, for being a true friend through all of it—I love experiencing the challenges and triumphs with you. SearchingForSunshine, for the sunset drinks that we'll have together someday.

The Book People

My agent, Emmanuelle Morgen, for believing so strongly in this project and our mission. You found the perfect home for this book, and I'm looking forward to many more adventures with you! My editor, Denise Silvestro, for filling this book with hope, and for genuinely believing the best in people—and also for leaving in every single reference to my cats.

The Happy People

Mom, for being the most inspiring and kind-hearted person in the world. Dad, for your unwavering support and for teaching me initiative. Doug and Lydia, for being great siblings and my best friends. My entire family, for lakehouse family dinners and the happiest memories ever. Tania, for making life beautiful again. Alex, for teaching me real love. Brian, for teaching me how to write. Ryan, for our productive days of writing (aka Super Smash Brothers). Doug, Becky, Brian, Joe, Erin, and Amy, for still being wonderful friends to me when I was insane.

The Cats

Nunc and Mosie, for bringing so much joy into our lives. Nelly, for his gay pride. Little Guy, for being the psychopath I'll always love.

Resources

As you educate yourself, information flow is essential. This is the time to get overloaded with knowledge, books, and videos. You'll find some that you like, and others that you don't. The important thing is, find a lot of them. Later on, you'll probably feel comfortable settling down with a few favorite resources, but now is the opportunity to try them all.

Our goal at Psychopath Free is to help you heal in the best way possible. That could be through this book and our site, or it could be through hundreds of other resources out there. This section is a rapid-fire way to get new survivors up to speed on how much information is available on the topic.

Search Terms

There are a lot of terms besides "psychopath" that might yield some very helpful resources. Here are some of the most common words that could help you in your search:

Psychopath
Sociopath
Narcissist

Narcissistic Personality Disorder (NPD)

Anti-Social Personality Disorder (ASPD)

Borderline Personality Disorder (BPD)

Emotional Abuse

Psychological Abuse

Psychological Maltreatment

Emotional Rape

Covert Abuse

Emotional Manipulator

Cluster B Personality Disorders

Psychopathology

Emotional Vampire

Websites

We do not necessarily endorse any of these sites or blogs, but we believe all survivors should have access to every resource out there. It is up to you to decide what helps or does not help your healing process.

PsychopathFree.com (articles and recovery forums)

PsychopathyAwareness.wordpress.com (blog and articles)

LoveFraud.com (blog, articles, and recovery forums)

DiscardedIndieMom.com (blog, articles)

NarcissismFree.com (articles)

SaferelationshipsMagazine.com (articles)

AlexandraNouri.com (articles)

DaughtersOfNarcissisticMothers.com (articles)

TheAbilityToLove.wordpress.com (articles)

Facebook Groups

Facebook groups and pages are an amazing way to connect with other survivors and validate your experience! Here are just a few, but you'll discover an entire community of them out there.

After Narcissistic Abuse—There is Light, Life, and Love
Narcissistic Abuse Recovery Central
Respite from Sociopathic Behavior
Psychopath Free
The Empathy Trap Book

Books

There are many books written on the topic of psychopathy. Check out some of our favorites, along with the most popular ones out there. Remember that not every resource will be right for you.

Dangerous Liaisons (Claudia Moscovici)
The Seducer (Claudia Moscovici)
The Sociopath Next Door (Martha Stout)
In Sheep's Clothing (George Simon)
Women Who Love Psychopaths (Sandra Brown)
How to Spot a Dangerous Man (Sandra Brown)
Without Conscience (Robert Hare)
Discarded (Indie Mom)
The Survivor's Quest (HealingJourney)
The Empathy Trap (Jane McGregor and Tim McGregor)

The Sociopath at the Breakfast Table (Jane McGregor and Tim McGregor)

Out of the FOG (Gary Walters)

The Smart Girl's Guide to Self-Care (Shahida Arabi)

Why Does He Do That?: Inside the Minds of Angry and Controlling Men (Lundy Bancroft)

Snakes in Suits (Paul Babiak)

Narcissistic Lovers (Cynthia Zayn)

The Wizard of Oz and Other Narcissists (Eleanor Payson)

Help! I'm In Love with a Narcissist (Steven Carter)

What Makes Narcissists Tick (Kathy Krajco)

Malignant Self-Love (Sam Vaknin)

Love Fraud (Donna Andersen)

Articles

For an extended collection of links, articles, and videos, please check out our master list—and feel free to contribute any that we missed:

Resources.PsychopathFree.com

Appendix

Psychopath Test

Psychopaths display a particular set of patterns in their relationships. This thirteen-question test can help you (or a friend) determine if you might be dating a toxic person.

For each question, add the corresponding answer number to your total score. For example, if you answer (1) to the first question and (4) to the second question, you have a total of 5 points so far. Then at the end, see which range your final score falls into. If you're bad at math like me, you can simply take the test online at Test.PsychopathFree.com, which will magically compute the results for you!

A. Does this person keep their promises?

1. Yes, of course. Whenever my partner makes a promise, I can be confident that they will follow through on it.

2. Sure, they usually keep their promises and their behavior aligns pretty closely with their words.

3. Sometimes. They're not very dependable, but they'll follow through on their words occasionally.

4. No, their actions never seem to match up with their sweeping words. I've mostly learned not to point it out, otherwise I seem sensitive and crazy.

B. Does your partner seem to understand your feelings?

1. They're very empathetic and compassionate! They always seem to understand where I'm coming from. If I ever bring up concerns, I know they'll listen and understand.

2. Not really, but it's always been this way. Even early on in the relationship, they were never especially caring. They can be pretty self-centered, but they're usually there for me if I really need help.

3. They're empathetic enough, and I don't need anything more.

4. Not anymore. I find myself desperately trying to explain how they might feel if they were in my shoes, but that just seems to annoy them. Or they give me the silent treatment. It makes me feel crazy.

C. Can this person be hypocritical?

1. They have never been hypocritical and they do not judge me for my mistakes. They don't believe they're above the rules.

2. If they are, I haven't noticed. We're all human after all.

3. At times, but they're able to admit fault when it's pointed out.

4. They seem to have extremely high expectations of me, but they behave as if those same standards don't apply to them.

D. Do they ever lie?

1. No, they would never lie to me.

2. No more so than any other person. White lies happen sometimes.

3. They lie every once in a while, but it doesn't seem malicious or intentional. If caught, they seem embarrassed and uncomfortable.

4. Yes, and nothing ever seems to be their fault. There's always an excuse for everything, even things that don't require excusing.

E. Does this person ever pull away or withhold affection?

1. No, my partner would never use these tactics in our relationship. If we ever have problems, we simply communicate them. We don't ignore one another and wait for someone to break the stalemate.

2. No, I don't get the sense they're pulling away or trying to avoid me. They might go quiet after an argument or something, but that's about it.

3. Sometimes, but it's been that way since the start of our relationship. It'd be nice to have consistency with my partner, but if I don't hear from them for a day, that's all right.

4. Yes, and it really confuses me after how attentive they were in the beginning of our relationship. It feels like they're constantly making excuses about why they can't communicate or spend time with me.

F. What about your feelings in the relationship?

1. I feel calm, peaceful, and safe in my relationship. It has been consistent since the start.

2. I'm mostly happy with my relationship and I know I can communicate with my partner if I have concerns.

3. I'm not very happy in the relationship, but I still feel comfortable expressing my opinions and frustrations.

4. I used to be such an easygoing person, but now I feel jealous, desperate, and needy all the time.

G. Are you afraid of losing this person?

1. Why would I ever worry about losing my partner? I know that our love is mutual, and that our relationship is healthy. This isn't even something that would enter my mind.

2. No, we both enjoy one another's company and share similar feelings about the relationship.

3. I'm not really 100 percent confident about our relationship, but I don't think they'd leave me.

4. Yes, after first showering me with praise and flattery, they suddenly seem reclusive and uninterested. I worry that any fight could be our last.

H. Do you trust your partner?

1. Absolutely, I would trust them with my life.

2. Sure, they don't do anything to make me distrust them.

3. Not really, because they seemed to change into a different person as time went on, so I never really knew what to expect.

4. No. I can't explain why, but I frequently find myself playing detective and digging into their claims.

I. Is there drama in your relationship?

1. We rarely ever get into arguments because we naturally understand how the other is feeling. We don't try to make each other jealous or create unnecessary tension. We're both striving to build trust with one another.

2. It's a regular amount of drama for any relationship. Nothing I haven't experienced with my other partners.

3. We argue a lot, but the same issues don't come up over and over again. However, I do wish I could be in a relationship with less fighting.

4. They said they hate drama, but there seems to be so much of it. We're always arguing about the same things. It feels like they're creating drama and then judging me for reacting to it.

J. How do they handle boredom?

1. They never get bored, and they enjoy spending time alone with their thoughts.

2. They get bored with mundane tasks, but don't we all?

3. They get bored pretty easily, but they don't mind spending periods of time on their own.

4. They're always bored and constantly seek attention from others.

K. What about their ex?

1. They never mentioned their ex and it's never been discussed in our relationship.

2. They're on good terms with their ex but they don't talk or communicate much, so it's not really an issue in our relationship.

3. They're friends with their ex and it makes me feel uncomfortable. But they've always been friends, so it's not my place to say anything.

4. They claim their "crazy" ex is jealous of us and I have nothing to worry about, but for some reason I suspect they're still talking. I feel like I'm always in competition with others for my partner's attention.

L. What was your relationship like in the beginning?

1. We were great friends. It didn't move too fast, we just made each other laugh and had fun together. All of my friends and family liked them a lot, and we've been happy together ever since.

2. Just like any other relationship starts. We got to know each other and had a bunch of things in common. Things have fizzled down since then, but we still like each other a lot. If there was a honeymoon phase, it certainly didn't consume my life.

3. Nothing special at first. We went on a few dates and I noticed some things that felt off (like maybe being rude to a waiter), but overall they seemed fine. The more we got to know each other, the more comfortable I became.

4. Life-consuming! Much more attentive than my previous partners. They seemed to have all the right things in common with me, implying we were perfect for each other. They texted me constantly and seemed infatuated by every single thing about me.

M. How does this person treat you?

1. They go above and beyond to listen to my feelings and understand where I'm coming from. I always feel respected in my relationship. If I bring up a concern, they're always willing to talk about it and improve their behavior to help our relationship.

2. Just like anyone else treats me. We joke around, have fun, and enjoy one another's company. We both treat each other like adults.

3. They're usually not very nice to me, but it's always been that way. I don't need a lot of affection or mushy kindness, so it's fine.

4. I don't even know anymore. We have good days, where it feels like the perfect beginning of our relationship again. But usually they're patronizing and critical, or they ignore me. I feel sensitive and crazy for being hurt by their behavior.

Results:

13–20: You Know a Genuinely Good Person!

Great news! This person seems like the complete opposite of a psychopath. They are empathetic, warm, and caring. Their intentions are genuine and their behavior reflects that. Wishing you a long and happy relationship!

21–30: They're Not a Psychopath

Good news! This person does not seem like a psychopath. You have ups and downs, just like any normal relationship. As long as you are happy, this is probably a healthy dynamic.

31–41: You Might Know a Psychopath

Be careful! There are some red flags about this person. They may or may not be a psychopath, but the bottom line is that you deserve to be in a relationship with someone who makes you happy. Someone who is empathetic, kind, and compassionate. Does this person embody those qualities?

42–52: You Definitely Know a Psychopath

Watch out! This person fits most of the traits of a psychopath. Are you constantly on edge around them? Did you go from feeling elated and joyful to anxious and frantic? Do they triangulate you with exes or other potential mates? Are you apologizing and crying more than you ever have in your life? Do you feel like you've lost your entire sense of self since the start of this relationship? Healthy, loving partners aren't supposed to make you feel bad about yourself. But with psychopaths, the abuse always starts after you're already hooked.

PsychopathFree.Com Survivor Survey Responses

Since the original Thirty Red Flags were published, they've been shared hundreds of thousands of times all over the Web. As the resource exploded in popularity, it was important to me that each red flag be accurate and validating to *all* survivors—not just a list of Jackson's experiences with the pronoun changed from "me" to "you."

And so, the closeted statistician in me put together an anonymous survey for survivors to rate each red flag on a scale of one to five, from "Strongly Disagree" to "Strongly Agree," along with a free response section for stuff I missed. I thought a dozen or so people might take the time to fill all this out and set me straight.

So you can only imagine my surprise when more than a thousand survivors stepped up to the plate to share their feedback. All red flags had a majority response of "Strongly Agree," which was absolutely shocking to me. But some rated slightly lower than others, so I was determined to reexamine those and make improvements for the new book. The updated red flags in this book are based directly on the most commonly mentioned phrases from a thousand survivors all around the world. And like anything else I write, they're always a work in progress, so I invite you to share your own feedback and criticisms at Survey.PsychopathFree.com.

Results:

Charted by weighted average, with Strongly Agree = 5
and Strongly Disagree = 1
Low X axis: Neutral = 3 (i.e., none of the red flags
averaged below 3.5, which is Neutral/Agree)
All red flags had majority response of "Strongly Agree"

Overall distribution. Strongly Agree: 59%, Agree: 22%,
Netural: 11%, Disagree: 5%, Strongly Disagree: 3%

Extracted Common Phrases from Free Responses:

Eroded my boundaries.

I groveled for forgiveness even though it was their fault.

Chameleon could fit into any situation.

Creates drama.

Abuse was subtle and covert.

Seemed amused at my worst.

I begged for them.

Stared blankly when I was hurt.

My life becomes complete chaos and confusion.

Mysterious childhood.

Father ignored them.

Mommy issues.

Alcohol and addiction.

No closure, sudden end.

Gossiped about me.

Control by hypnosis and neuro-linguistic programming.

Flirting/triangulating with everyone.

They became my entire life and I was isolated.

Invokes pity and sympathy.

Word salad arguments made no sense.

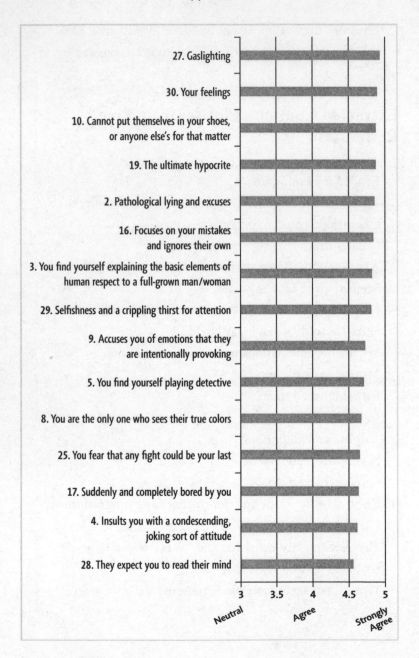

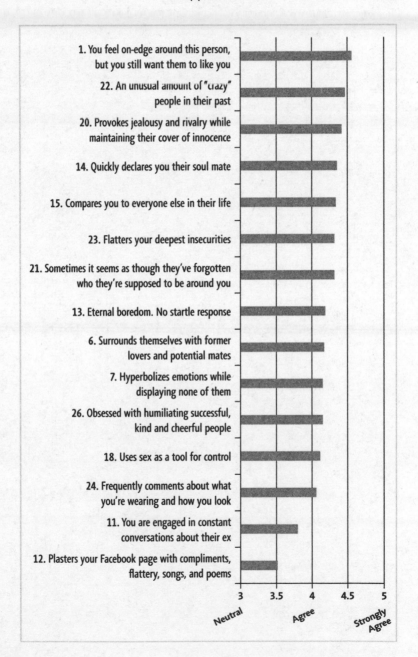

1. You feel on-edge around this person, but you still want them to like you

22. An unusual amount of "crazy" people in their past

20. Provokes jealousy and rivalry while maintaining their cover of innocence

14. Quickly declares you their soul mate

15. Compares you to everyone else in their life

23. Flatters your deepest insecurities

21. Sometimes it seems as though they've forgotten who they're supposed to be around you

13. Eternal boredom. No startle response

6. Surrounds themselves with former lovers and potential mates

7. Hyperbolizes emotions while displaying none of them

26. Obsessed with humiliating successful, kind and cheerful people

18. Uses sex as a tool for control

24. Frequently comments about what you're wearing and how you look

11. You are engaged in constant conversations about their ex

12. Plasters your Facebook page with compliments, flattery, songs, and poems

3   3.5   4   4.5   5

Neutral   Agree   Strongly Agree